HAUTE DISH

VOICES OF RESILIENCE

OLEB
Books

Oleb Books
6417 Penn Avenue S.
STE 7-1419
Minneapolis, MN 55423
https://www.olebbooks.com/

Managing Editor: Stephanie Major
Assistant Editor: Kit Renard
Copyeditors: James Estwick and Anna Stagg
Book Designer: Monkey C Media
First Edition

Published in the United States of America
ISBN: 979-8-9897474-3-6 (paperback)
ISBN: 979-8-9897474-4-3 (ebook)
Library of Congress Control Number: 2026936680

The editors of *Haute Dish* dedicate our inaugural anthology to Metropolitan State University emeritus professor Alison McGhee. In founding the Creative Writing Bachelor of Arts program on campus, she created a haven for budding writers. Her belief in the power of words teaches us that resilience takes root on the page and blossoms far beyond it. Just as the monarch butterfly relies on the resolute milkweed for refuge and renewal, so too do Metro's students thrive in the supportive environment she created. This anthology is a tribute to her belief that every person has a story to share. Thank you, Professor McGhee, for the enrichment and vibrancy you continue to bring to the Metro State Community.

CONTENTS

Part II: MEMOIR / 39

FOREWORD

You, dear reader, are a resilient person.

Perhaps you know this to be true for yourself. Perhaps you're doubting, thinking: me, resilient?

It can be easy to shrug off the pride and mantle of such a weighty, important word. But, if you are doubting, know this: By way of human nature, if you are still here, you are resilient.

You have met situations meant to break you, and you did not break. Or you did break, and you mended. Or you didn't fully mend, but you're here all the same, persisting with the parts of you that are left.

Our students and alumni will share their resiliency with you in the following pages. Through poetry, personal essays, and short stories, they will guide you through those moments that were meant to break them. Some were a lightning strike to the heart, splitting a life into before and after. Some are a testament to moving through a world built around systems that were never designed for their success or acceptance. Some are about rebuilding a life that was torn down to brass tacks. These talented writers have demonstrated strength and courage in their vulnerability, telling us in turn what it means that *they are still here.*

And you, reader, are still here.

We are all still here.

And thus, since we are here together, we shall embark on a journey through the pages, allowing us to witness the profound resilience found at Metro State University. My hope is that your journey will be similar to mine as I read through these breathtaking pieces. Page after page, I found my empathy expanded and my own sense of resilience strengthened.

I hope you, too, feel connected to the roots of your humanity, as I did. We know history because of the survivors and the storytellers. And one thing is true throughout the ages: There is the survival of an ordeal, and then there is the feast. This is our feast.

This anthology is a culmination of years of hard work, the organization itself forged through resilience. Professor Suzanne Nielsen founded *Haute Dish* in 2004. Over the decades it endured, thanks to the work of many committed and passionate volunteers. Each of the students who worked on Haute Dish in these twenty-one years have stayed the course through their own struggles, personal and academic, to ensure a successful printing and distribution each semester.

Thanks to that growth and dedication, *Haute Dish* is now expanding into new territory. In your hands is the first annual anthology.

This anthology represents the true gift of resilience: that when we persist in showing up, even if only with those parts of ourselves that were still left standing after the storm, and when we choose to face challenges with hard work and determination, doors can and will open in rewarding and remarkable ways.

And so, dear, resilient reader, let us now commence this journey. Perhaps you will see yourself in these pages. Perhaps you will find the inspiration to grow beyond who you are today. Perhaps you will rest in the most important and essential takeaway of this anthology:

You are still here.

Thank you for still being here. Thank you for showing up and sharing this moment with us.

Let's feast.

Sincerely,
Stephanie Major
Managing Editor

PART I: POETRY

I'm Staying Right Here

Eponine Diatta

When I walk down the street, you better lock your doors
Guard your purses and clutch your pearls
Yeah, I see your body tensin'
Cuz I just touched down on your block
On the other side of the white picket fencin'

You gasp and cross the street
When you see me pass by, why?
I'm scary no matter what I do
Trust me, I've tried

I'd hunch down into a ball
Tried to make myself small
I'd quiet my voice down
Sing real soft while you're around
Hot irons and chemical burns,
Silk presses and perms
I tried
Smoothin' the kinks out my hair
Things that made me different
Made me scary
I buried it deep down there.
But you still run, you still hide
You still shut the blinds
Draw lines
Pick up the phone and dial the blues
A thousand times

You still take the steel off the mantle
Put your finger on the trigger
Chase me down
Run me outta town
Shoot me dead and leave me
Bleeding on the ground

I see now, the scary thing about me
Is me

So close your windows, lock your doors
Grab your Glock, call the cops
On your block, in your city, in every state you been to
I'm staying right here
If anyone's leaving
Then let it be you

Eponine (Nina) Diatta is in her first year at Metro State as a Professional Communications major. She is a multidisciplinary writer and performer who, in her free time, can be found hogging the TouchTunes at dive bars across the Twin Cities.

Breathe Again

Jordan Cooper

Forgive.
Forget?
How do I begin this climb—bare hands scraping stone,
lungs burning with memory?

The mountain was not made of stone,
but of what you left behind—the words, the silence,
the ache that still echoes.

Is forgiveness to say,
"There was no wrong,"
"It doesn't scar me,"
or *"It simply never happened"*?

Maybe it means
I'm moving forward,
leaving your shadow
in the valley below.

I will climb these jagged rocks.
The wind will sting my eyes.
I will stumble,
I will fall,
and still—I will rise.

Because someday,
I will reach the summit—muscles trembling,
heart alive.

And there,
in the thin air,
I will learn
to breathe again,
celebrating life.

Jordan Cooper is an English for Teaching major in their first year at Metro State. Their work often explores survival, growth, and vulnerability, making this publication especially meaningful.

Expectations

Paula Foreman

On a December afternoon, well below freezing,
I drive to the construction site,
leave the car beside a barricade of cedar boards,
totter over the frozen mud ruts to the foreman's trailer,
and knock on the door to ask for a job,
pending my graduation
from stay-at-home parent to single mom.
The building trades pay better than offices where,
this being the '80s,
women are required to strangle
their legs in pantyhose and breathe recycled air as stale
as the coffee.
The union hall agent hands me a reference served with a smirk.
Every man knows no one hires in December and,
this being the '80s,
they all are men.
The foreman, his barreled torso
made massive by layers of Carhartt, fills the doorway
and growls,
Do you have any experience?
though he can tell I don't.
He studies his applicant
in her blue jeans, tan corduroy blazer, brown loafers.
Can you start Monday?
I return to the union hall to report my hiring,
surprising the guy who sent me, who cackled at a girl who
thinks she's tough.
The boys will find out I do have experience.

Marriage and childbirth taught me something about pain, long hours,
and the lowered expectations of men.

Paula Foreman has been writing since she could hold a pencil. She lives in St. Paul with her husband, who helps her farm, and her border collie Cedar, who doesn't.

Decay

Hawthorne Fasching

The envelope is pushed ever further
no one to care enough to save you
humanity's crushing weight above you
heightened expectations linger below
no one to save you
not a soul to care

Perhaps someone would notice
were you to die, pause and mourn at your bedside
remember the bitter life you sired
your grand dreams dashed by a reaper's knife
adorn their mourning gowns
set their sleepy town ablaze with rage

But fire on fire only leads to more destruction
a life left behind, unfulfilled, hardly even lived
is not a life, but a miserable existence
cold and empty, ever dying in lifeless hands
when the earth decays, as do you
fertilizing her roots, you hope to start anew

And perhaps that will not save her
or stop their blood from staining the streets
but peace will forever take you
ever present, sinking in deep
the ones who love you will still weep

Hawthorne Fasching is in his third year of studies as an English and History major at Metropolitan State University. He spends his days drafting his novel and hanging out with his cats, and can often be found volunteering and powerlifting.

Toll

Carter Nodes

The ringing
Sings through air of
Fog and mist.
Gray permeates,
Holds, still,
Through night unrelenting.
I am spirit,
I am fog,
I am the mist who
Carries along
The slipstreams that
Coat the streets beneath.
My feet skip
Stones, over murky
Flooding waters who
Drown city streets.
Homes, engorged into this
Vortex of volatility.
Torn from reality and
Into something
Misunderstood.
Gliding now,
I surf o'er the
Muddled waters and
At the steps
Of a great castle.
Who stands tall,
Foreboding.

Her arches leading
Towards a sorrowful sky.
Who knows not
What to answer.
Her doors open,
Dust billows out,
Salting the water.
It is dark,
The light has faded.
All sight has retreated.
For where would dark be
If not where I stood.

Carter Nodes graduated from Metro State University in 2025 with a Bachelor's Degree in Psychology and a minor in Creative Writing. Carter can be found writing, boxing, or even writing about boxing! While a poet at heart, Carter also dabbles in horror and lengthier noire dramas.

I Am

Alexander Kelly

I am not,
and yet
I am.
A drop in the ocean
is still the ocean.
A grain of sand
is still the desert.
But losing a drop does not dry
the ocean.
And though the wind steals
the sand,
it cannot steal
the desert.
The grain will find the desert,
as the rain returns the drop.
The ocean moves
as it pleases.
The desert dances
in the wind.
The Source does not lose,
it gives.
I am not,
and yet
I am.

Alexander Kelly is a junior at Metro State studying Psychology. Alexander lives in the Twin Cities and enjoys going for walks, playing piano, and spending time with family.

Alchemy

Amber Honeycutt

Dirty,
a heavy wound.
Limbs tangle and bang into one another.
And always, there are the memories.
A gunshot under my skin.
Rearing their heads,
fangs striking through the empty spaces of my mind.

Cords wrapped around my wrists,
sticks and blades find their way to unspeakable places.
I have felt darkness.

It has slithered into me,
woven its way through muscle,
burrowed through bone and seeped through marrow.
It wrapped my mind in thick blankets,
shot like fire down my neurons.
I could not tell it apart from joy.

But I snuck through the cracks in the wall,
slunk behind smoke screens.
My quiet was the loudest roar I've ever heard.
I stared down the barrel into the black eyes of death,
 and whispered that I am not afraid.

It welled in my stomach,
burst through the hollow of my chest,

soared past my lips,
hanging in the air like an exclamation point.

Bad times to bad habits to buried truths,
connecting the dots eternally,
never quite finding the picture.

When gravity is too strong for me to stand,
I hold the earth with clenched fists.
If my strength cannot be drawn from the wonders of the sky,
I will rip it from the blackest of soils.

Amber Honeycutt is in her second year at Metro State, studying Computer Science. She spends her free time painting, writing, enjoying nature, going to concerts, or curling up with a good book.

Streetsong

Gregory Pickett

I learned to sleep beneath the moon.
When winter bit the bone,
the streets became my lullaby,
the shadows were my home.

At sixteen years, I lost my key,
the world forgot my name,
I wrapped myself in concrete dreams,
and whispered off the shame.

The buses hummed like holy hymns,
the alleys spoke in code,
each dawn a test, each dusk a prayer,
to walk another road.

I begged for warmth, I stole for bread,
I bartered truth for lies,
but somewhere deep beneath the ache,
a small light would not die.

It flickered when I found a meal,
or laughed beneath the rain.
It hummed inside my
hollow chest,
and soothed the edge of pain.

The cops would move me block to block,
the shelters came and went,
but I held fast to one belief—
that life was not yet spent.

And years would pass like falling leaves,
the frost became my friend,
until the day I looked around
and saw the tunnel's end.

Now when I see the houseless souls,
I do not look away,
I nod as if to tell them this:
You will survive the day.

For walls and roofs can fall apart,
and money turns to flame,
but still the heart remembers how
to rise and start again.

Gregory Pickett is in his second year at Metro State University. He lives in Loring Park in Minneapolis next to a beautiful pond where he contemplates how many hours of video games he's played in his 45 years of life.

What the Fire Did Not Burn

Gregory Pickett

I have seen angels with backpacks,
three little girls who walk the halls
like sunlight wrapped in bruises,
who color the corners of trauma
with broken crayons and quiet songs.

They do not tell me everything.
They do not have to.
Their eyes already carry
what the body cannot say.
But still, they smile
like children who refuse to surrender
their right to joy.

The oldest ties her sister's shoes.
The middle one hums under her breath,
a melody too strong to die.
The youngest still believes
that magic is hiding in the pencil box,
waiting to draw them free.

And I,
a man learning how to listen,
stand between their laughter and the storm.
I wish I could pull the hurt out of the air,
name it, crush it,
make the world apologize.

But resilience is not mine to give.
It blooms inside them
like spring through concrete,
like breath through the ashes.

One day they will tell their story
and the earth will stop to hear it.
One day they will laugh so loud
that the monster will vanish
beneath the sound of their living.

For now, they learn, they play,
they draw the sun again and again,
and I swear
the light they make
is enough to heal the sky.

*Gregory Pickett is in his second year at Metro State University.
He lives in Loring Park in Minneapolis next to a beautiful pond
where he contemplates how many hours of video games he's played
in his 45 years of life.*

Seasons

Mandy Vue

These days the weather has grown cold, the land changing into the shades of fall.
When I look at the changing colors, I am often reminded of you.
Your presence, lingering constantly on my mind,
As if you're dancing, surrounding yourself within my thoughts,
A fog that I am slipping into between a dreamlike state and reality.
If I could turn back time, I would be a better daughter.
I would love you harder, hold you closer.
I think about your garden and the abundance of love and effort you put in to feed your children.
Your small hands, rough, strong, and full of calluses.
The hands who raised us to be resilient, to keep our wits, to become our own.
I have grown into my own woman over these years.
A reflection of who you used to be.
I am like you in so many ways and forms.
Sometimes I even catch glimpses of you in myself.
I am your daughter after all.
As the season changes and the years pass by, I will forever carry you in my heart.
I love you always, my dearest mother.
These are the words I wish I could tell you one last time.

Mandy Vue is in her fourth year at Metro State on the Individualized Studies track with a focus on Leadership in Business Management and Operations. She enjoys reading and writing poetry, cooking, binge-watching shows, and traveling.

Enough

Anna Stagg

Oh to refrain from making my place in this world,
from shouting my name from the mountaintop,
from wondering if they know the uniqueness of me;
and if they do, could it be that
I'm not
    enough?

Oh to put aside the cares of man,
to walk in secrecy.
To shut my mouth in the cleft of the rock,
to marvel that you see me.
Oh to be okay that only you—
and to love that you do—
know me intimately.

Oh the rest my soul finds when my mind stops running to
shout on that mountaintop!
To be heard, to be loved,
to be noticed, to be
proven.

Oh the angst this has brought my heart.
Oh the peace that your knowing me imparts
when I'm content with secrecy, for
you are
    enough
for me.

Anna Stagg will graduate from Metro State this spring with a BA in Individualized Studies and a minor in Creative Writing. She lives in Minneapolis with her husband and two of her four adult children.

I'm Just Tired

Sumaya Khaliif

I'm trapped and I can't breathe.
Carrying this weight all alone is breaking me.
I can feel parts of me cracking,
Yet I can't tell where the sound leads.

This ongoing cycle that never seems to end,
For how long must I be expected to not shed
Emotions, tears, blood, and sweat,
Things I must conceal all for comfort.

But what about mine?
I wish for the same,
It just feels as if none of this applies to me.
The kind of care, love, and gentleness,
I watched it all drift past me.

Knowing me, I chased it all my life,
Like a kid trying to run after their own shadow.
Yet where has that ever led me?
Smiling, with tears in my eyes.

The mask is torn and should be released.
Let the true me be exposed for the world to see.
Let her be embraced for who she can be.
Hold her heart, and tell her she can be free,
Free from expectations and convenience.

Why hold her back when she can be so much more?
Remove her from this box you so desperately keep her in.
Untie her wings, let her fly.
Give her a chance,
And perhaps she'll soar.

Sumaya Khaliif is in her third year at Metro State University, studying Communication. She spends her days reflecting, journaling, reading, and finding ways to be the best version of herself. She enjoys long walks and loves to laugh until her eyes water.

More Than

Julian Zuk

A single choice, no matter when,
Becomes the lens they see me in.
They claim I'm free, but not to stray.
This cage just changed its form, not way.

Invisible walls still block my climb,
Though healing lessons once were mine.
Probation says, I must leave them behind.
The very tools that healed my mind.

Be grateful now, they softly chide,
"Or we can just throw you back inside."
Freedom's thin, when chains still stay,
One misstep, and it's all stripped away.

A life condemned, a dream displaced,
Relentless fires, patiently faced.
From ashes scarred, my voice will rise,
Forged by trials only I realize.

I've stumbled, fallen, borne regret,
But rising now shows I'm stronger yet.
I study, serve, extend my hand,
To lift the bruised, help them withstand.

I am not fear, nor label's weight,
Not just the sum of past mistakes.

Though judged, confined, denied my right,
I'll turn my scars into maps of light.

So, brand me felon, curse my name,
You'll only fan these unyielding flames.
I wear my scars, but not your shame,
A beacon shining through the flame.
To guide the lost from night's cold turn,
And light a path where harm can't return.

Julian Zuk is a senior studying Transformative Justice whose academic work is shaped by his lived experiences navigating stigma, conditional freedom, and the possibilities of accountability and healing. His journey informs his commitment to reimagining justice through empathy, vulnerability, and community support.

In Honor of Marines Lost

Brian Volkmuth

Since the birth of our nation, defenders have been needed.
Our loyalty to country and each other was seeded.
The fires of freedom forged the first Marines.

Born in Tun Tavern, filled with esprit de corps,
Our history is rife with heroes, honor, and war,
Each forged into the metal that makes new Marines.

Their names and hometowns are unknown to me.
In our youth, we chose the same path to seek.
To defend our Nation, we became Marines.

The costs of these battles are my Sisters and Brothers.
My prayers I send to their families, fathers, and mothers.
Now God will take care of our Marines.

The hands of these souls I did not hold.
Their struggles and pain, I need not be told.
These we know, for we are all Marines.

As memories of battles and heroes are lost,
I pray we all keep fresh the cost
Of all these brave and valiant Marines.

Semper Fi!

*Brian Volkmuth is a Marine Corps veteran and has been a tenured
faculty member at St. Cloud Technical & Community College since*

2013. He holds a BS in Information Assurance from Metro State University, where he is currently a DBA student. He is a married father of seven children and has ten grandchildren.

The Shape of Survival

Jordan Cooper

I grieve—for that which is lost.
I hope—for what is yet to come.
I hurt—as I remember
what he took,
what he did,
what can never be made right,
and I am forever changed.

Because now—*I know the truth.*
The world is dark,
my innocence gone,
my trust betrayed,
my mind fractured.

The world—is full of pain,
full of lies,
full of evil.

But he cannot define me.

I stand.
I speak.
I hope.
I live.
I choose peace.

In this moment, *I believe—*
that I matter,
that I have value *apart from him.*

Though he has broken me,
I can rebuild.

I have **survived.**
I am **strong.**
I will **grow.**

Jordan Cooper is an English for Teaching major in their first year at Metro State. Their work often explores survival, growth, and vulnerability, making this publication especially meaningful.

Messages

Michael Yer Vang

Monday: Hey man, remember that show we used to watch
as kids?
Message seen.

Tuesday: I know we haven't talked in a while, but we always
picked up where we left off.
Message seen.

Wednesday: I just want to know what you've been up to; I see
you started a family.
Message seen.

Thursday: I hope you're happy.
Message seen.

Friday: But it always pisses me off how I always contact you
first, and you never answer.
Right there under your name it says "Active Now" and all I
want is little acknowledgement.
Just let me know that I exist.
Fourteen years we've been friends and all I see is "Message
seen."

I share with you something that makes me laugh and you don't
engage with me.
Is it because you're afraid of this disability? Of my epilepsy?
Does that make you scared of me?
You don't want to be seen with me because you don't want to

see me convulsing on the floor?
Is that the reason why I was never invited anymore?
Why we lost this connection?

At least treat me with some dignity and tell me why.

Your non-response compresses my brain like an old, wrinkled
scrap of paper,
it's worse than my hydrocephalus.
So toss it in the fire and let it burn.
Let those ashes fly in the wind like the friends we used to be.

I won't even say goodbye; I've wasted enough of my time.
Message failed to send.

*Michael Yer Vang is a senior at Metro State who plans to graduate
with a double major in English and Creative Writing in the
summer of 2026. When not studying, he spends his time at home
reading, wondering, writing, and trying to figure out what to do
next.*

PART II: MEMOIR

How to Skip Your Best Friend's Funeral

Mickey Mahoney

The day after you find out she's dead, drive five hours from your gig to her hometown. That's Decorah, Iowa, to Grand Rapids, Minnesota. Sleep on Jesse and Cierra's floor. Watch *Eternal Sunshine of the Spotless Mind.* Listen to them talk about the cinematography, the thought that went into every shot while you stare at an imperfect angle from the floor. When the shitheads show up, slumped pale, and still rolling, try to be empathetic. Feel sick when Cade says they finished off her drugs. Feel sick when Sara says she's going to throw drugs in the casket. Feel sick when Jesse says, without saying, that it's her fault; she could never let anything go. Say no to the joint, say no to the wine. Step out for a cigarette with Cierra, feel sick. Feel sick when she shows you the picture of your friend's body, lifeless in the hospital. Go to sleep but don't dream, she will not be there.

In the morning, ride with Jesse and Cade to the woods. They'll tell you it was her favorite spot. Suddenly, you'll see her everywhere. Cade will catch you smiling and snap your picture. Now you'll never forget the silence between your teeth. The river says it will never hold her again. You'll picture her there with wings. You'll hear her laugh and turn to look for her face in the trees. You'll admit to yourself, no; you'll try to picture her gone, but that would mean picturing her gone, and that requires a wild imagination. Your heart will become a body bracing for impact. The sky, as heavy as nothing, hurls toward you. You'll want to cry, but instead you'll ask about the funeral. They'll have to fly her body home from California; that will take a while.

Something about documenting overdoses in California. You'll picture her again, with wings.

Driving back to Minneapolis, you'll remember it's June. You'll remember your birthday is in five days. You'll be turning twenty-three. You'll remember her golden birthday would have been November 25th. You'll remember meeting her for the first time at church camp. You were nine, then ten, then eleven, twelve, thirteen. You'll scan the decade, blurred by tears. You'll turn the windshield wipers on and laugh at yourself. You'll remember the church. The way you two dreamt of leaving, finally free. You'll remember two months before, sitting with her at a bar in Northeast Minneapolis. She said she was clean. You'll remember six months before that, the bruises on her arms as you moved her out of her ex-husband's house. Remember he was the son of preacher, blaming her for everything his God wasn't.

When Cade calls to tell you the funeral is at her home church, that her home pastor will give the service, feel sick. Say no. Emphatically, angrily. When he tells you about her sisters, all four of them, he'll say the youngest keeps asking for her. That her parents blame her exodus, said she died when she left God. Hold back the tears, but not the truth. Say fuck them and drive instead, eighteen hours, to a music festival in New York. Say it's what she wanted. Tell yourself she would have hated her funeral; she wouldn't be caught dead at that church. Go instead to the music festival, where you only like one band. Get too fucked up. Sleep all day. Cheat with your ex. Excuse your behavior. Watch the one band. Remember that your best friend is dead. Stare at the lake. Try to cry. Try to dream. Ask her to appear anywhere. Look for her everywhere. Take stimulant after stimulant, drive eighteen hours back home. Stop once at 5:00 a.m. Sleep on the grass outside a rest stop somewhere around Ohio. Ignore the calls. Ignore the texts. Believe you're fine, stronger even. Ask for a picture of her tombstone. Delete the picture. Feel sick. Get home, ignore your roommates. They won't understand. No one will understand. At some point you'll realize that your birthday has passed. You don't remember it at all.

Years will go by, slower than they ever have before. You'll try to write about her, you'll try to write to her. You'll try to sing, which is to say you'll search for a melody to wrap around this gaping wound, your mouth cracked with all its failures to soothe. You'll mistake grief for needlessness, delete all her texts and photos. Regret is nothing, if not for later. You'll lose your grandpa, but that will feel easier. Your mom will move away. Your sister will go into treatment. You'll lose lovers and friends, and for a time you will be too scared to love again.

For a while, she will star in your dreams. You will see her and say, "I can't believe you've been alive this whole time," and then you'll wake up, write it down. Try to remember what she looks like. Try to picture her old. Wonder what you would argue about today, if she would like your partner. If you two would have fallen in love. Wonder if you were in love. Feel grief all over again, all over again being the sixth stage of grief. Grief being a stage, your heart a spotlight, never enough the play, too much the audience. No, the play before, the audience after. You skipped the funeral. Now, find the words. Find the words out there; they must be with her somewhere.

Mickey Mahoney is a junior at Metro State University, studying Creative Writing. They live in Minneapolis with their partner and an extremely spoiled cat. When they aren't writing poetry, Mickey is playing bass and touring the world with bands made up of their best friends.

The Christmas Rug

Tara Flaherty Guy

Lacy snowflakes are starting to swirl down as I thumb through the mail on my way into the house from the mailbox. I'm startled to see a Christmas card from Matt in the mix, with an unfamiliar return address. He's never been a card-sender, so my curiosity is piqued. I haven't seen my friend and former coworker since … when? Two birthdays ago at least. Since retiring I've only seen my old office pals on special occasions, but the sparkly red envelope makes me think of all the Christmases I spent with them—my office family and best friends for decades. The years reel away as I remember one Christmas with Matt in particular.

*****

My coworkers had launched into their annual holiday depredations and decorated my office, I discovered upon my return after my Thanksgiving week away. It looked like some tasteless, dyspeptic Santa had crept in and vomited Yuletide cheer all over my desk. I laughed out loud—the desired response—at the sheer crappiness of the décor as they gathered at my cubicle door to get my reaction.

"You know if you run out on us on decorating day, you get whatever's left in the bottom of the box," Jackie said, laughing. We had all worked together for decades, and over those years we'd amassed a collection of beat-up, cast-off Christmas decorations that would shame even the tackiest rummage sale.

I looked around at the execrable collection: a prehistoric artificial Christmas tree that appeared to be fashioned out of green toilet brushes, chipped and sparkly reindeer, elves and angels, a lascivious-looking elf-on-the-shelf, a battered nutcracker, a mangy partridge in a spindly pear tree, and a little Irish Santa hanging from my coat hook as though garroted. A pink-tinted, heavily shellacked manger scene caught my eye. I peered at the tiny plaque at its base, which announced it had been carved from Spam, then burst out laughing.

"In the spirit of this meat-Nativity thing, Jesus Christ, what have you done?" Another burst of laughter, then the hilarity slowly dissolved as everyone wandered away to begin the workday.

At midmorning when I came back from refilling my coffee, I noticed a garish latch-hooked rug hanging on the outside of my cubicle. It depicted a bright green Christmas tree studded with genuine gold jingle bells on a field of fire-engine red, trimmed with faux ermine. *Good God*, I thought, *what an abomination*. The round rug measured about a yard in diameter and was hanging by a crocheted gold cord. I hadn't seen a latch-hooked rug since my grandmother used to fashion the craft show favorites, trying to keep her arthritic fingers nimble. It was old lady art.

"Horrible, isn't it?" asked a deep voice behind me. I turned to find Matt standing there looking at the kitschy display, a melancholy smile on his face.

"Are you the perpetrator?" I asked, laughing. "I would have thought you had better taste, somehow."

"Yep, that was mine. Marissa has permanently bequeathed it to the office for all eternity ... although 'banished it from the house' would be closer to the truth," he said.

"I definitely would have thought 'she' had more refined sensibilities," I said, thinking of his stiff and snooty wife. I tried to picture it hanging anywhere in their big, beautifully appointed home and failed.

"She does. That's why it's here now."

A friend for 20 years, Matt was like my little brother, but I only knew his wife Marissa in a chilly, distant way. We were a tightknit work group, but unlike the other office spouses who gathered good-naturedly for the requisite holiday parties, Marissa scorned our society, which meant that Matt had to fly solo if he wanted to attend. He had finally confessed years ago, when her myriad excuses wore too thin to be believed, that she just didn't like us. As far as I could tell, she didn't like anyone, not even Matt. He had been coming to our office gatherings without her for years.

"My mom made it for our first married Christmas," he said, face averted. I saw a flush creeping from his neck to his face, as his jaw tensed and flexed. "Ten years ago. It's been in the attic ever since."

I was appalled. Not that Marissa consigned the thing to the attic, but because Matt's mother had died suddenly not even a full month ago. He had been close to his mom, despite the fact that his wife was deeply antagonistic to their relationship. That Marissa would—not even a month after the old lady died—purge their house of a gift that she had labored over caused something to crack a little bit near my heart.

"Wow," I breathed. "That is monumentally shitty."

Matt dug the toe of his work boot into the carpet. When he looked up, his eyes were glistening. "Is it?" he asked quietly. "It's hard to tell when you're in it. But I thought so too … on the bright side, at least I don't have to choose between Mom and her this Christmas Eve."

I rose wordlessly and went to him, put my arms around him and hugged him. "You deserve better, hon. You know this, right?"

"I guess," he mumbled into my hair. "At least I thought my mom did."

I hugged him harder. "You both do, Matty."

With a final squeeze and whispered thanks, he wandered away, shoulders sagging.

*****

Brushing snow from my hair, I drop the mail on my kitchen counter. Slitting open the envelope, I draw out Matt's Christmas card and read the cramped printing inside.

Hey sista,

Merry Christmas! Miss you—let's grab a beer soon. Meantime, I thought you'd wanna know—I reclaimed it. It's hanging on the door to my new digs—come see it. Thanks for helping me figure out that I did deserve better ... and that Mom's gift did too.

Matt

I slide the photo out of the envelope. There is the latch-hooked rug in all its dubious splendor, hanging on the door of Apartment #32.

Tara Flaherty Guy obtained her BA in Creative Writing in 2018 from Metro State University in St. Paul, where she was born and raised, and still lives and writes. Since then, her work has been published in St. Paul Almanac, Remington Review, Emerge Literary Journal, and Longridge Review, among many others.

Labyrinth of Shadows:
The Stillness Between Fire and Flight

Tasbiha Hasan

2024 was the year that broke me. 2025 became the year that healed me, between them stretched a landscape of fire and flight, stillness and surrender, faith, and becoming. Each season reshaped me as though I were walking through a myth written in light, stone, and wings.

I. The Phoenix: Rising from Ashes

The year opened with embers. I carried the weight of unfinished work and a gnawing voice that whispered, *maybe you are not enough*. I had lost confidence and almost lost belief in myself. But the ashes did not end me; they became my soil. Somewhere beneath the spot, a spark waited. When I returned from Pakistan that December and stepped into a new semester, I made a quiet promise: I will rise again, even if I rise slowly. The phoenix in me awoke when I dared to begin anew. Each small commitment felt like lighting a match in the dark. When tiny victories arrived, I cried not because they proved anything to anyone, but because they reminded me that beginnings are still possible. Rebirth, I learned, is not loud. It is a whisper that says, *try again*.

II. The Dragon: Guarding My Dreams

Spring became the season of fire. Tasks multiplied; deadlines collided. I spent long nights wrestling with data, theory, and doubts. The dragon rose from fierce fatigue but disciplined. It taught me to defend my time, focus, and peace. I learned that saying no can be an act of devotion. I protected my dreams as something sacred. Courage, I realized, isn't the absence of exhaustion; it is showing up even when exhausted.

III. The Crane: Balancing Strength and Stillness

By summer, I needed wings more than armor. The dragon's roar quieted into the crane's calm. Balance came slowly. Morning tea became reflection; evening walks became prayer. For someone who had spent months proving herself, stillness felt rebellious. Yet that stillness birthed clarity: success without peace is only half a victory. The crane reminded me that balance is not achieved once it is practiced daily.

IV. Medusa: The Season of Stone

Then came the shadow. Loneliness and fatigue returned. I often thought Medusa misunderstood, vilified, yet powerful. Like her, I turned inward, shielding myself behind silence. My emotions hardened into stone, not out of anger but protection. Even stone holds memory. I found solace in reflection, in writing about resilience, in quiet faith. Strength sometimes means allowing yourself to break and trusting that the cracks will one day shine. Medusa taught me empathy for myself and for anyone who hides pain behind grace.

V. The Caterpillar: The Stillness of Becoming

Autumn arrived quietly. The fire dimmed, the stone softened, and I withdrew into stillness. Like a caterpillar, I cocooned, slow, introspective, deliberate. I trimmed commitments, choosing depth over speed. I learned that retreating is not regression; sometimes the most important growth happens when no one sees it.

Inside that cocoon, I began weaving a new philosophy: a five-step promise to myself. I would break every task into the smallest possible parts until progress felt gentle. I would shorten the distance to my north star instead of chasing it endlessly. I would live by balance—by the power of 50/50.

VI. The Butterfly: Emergence

Winter returned with quiet joy. The cocoon opened slowly, and wings unfolded delicate but determined. I was no longer only surviving deadlines; I was creating meaning. My words and actions carried both science and soul. I began to share my story not as perfect but as proof that transformation is possible. The butterfly reminded me that fragility and power can coexist. Alhamdulillah (All praise and thanks be to God) for every version of myself that had made flight possible.

VII. 2025 Integration and the Power of 50/50

If 2024 was the year that broke me open, 2025 would be the year that taught me to live whole. Healing did not come as a sudden sunrise. It arrived softly through consistency, faith, and gratitude. I rebuilt my habits, replacing chaos with clarity, perfectionism with patience. I stopped chasing extremes and began practicing balance. Ten months into my resolution, it still holds strong not because everything is easy, but because I've learned to meet life halfway through.

This year, I entered new spaces: business-startup proposals, research-presentation opportunities, and competitions whose results are still pending. There have been rejections and small triumphs, but I've learned not to measure myself only by outcomes. The point is, I'm participating. I'm showing up for my own life. The power of 50/50 became my compass: half discipline, half grace; half drive, half rest. It keeps me steady through the unknown.

VIII. The Power of Duality

There were tears, there was laughter, and there was balance, the rhythm of it all. As November approaches, I joke about not "jinxing" my progress, but deep down I know the truth: learning itself is the reward. I am no longer just the Bambi I once was, nor only the Medusa who guarded her pain. I honor both the innocence that kept me tender and the strength that taught me to look directly at life. The butterfly in me ensures that softness survives, while the Medusa in me protects it. Perhaps that's what growth truly means, earning the switch between gentleness and power, between vulnerability and mystery. I call it the power of duality, the quiet assurance that I can be kind and commanding, soft and unshakable, human and whole. Alhamdulillah (all praise and thanks be to God) for this balance for the mystery that makes life alluring, and for the strength that makes it worth living.

Tasbiha Fatima Hasan is a senior undergraduate student at Metropolitan State University, expected to graduate in 2026. She is passionate about sustainability, data analytics, and research, and continues to build a multidisciplinary portfolio through academic projects, leadership roles, and creative work.

Beyond the Scarlet Letter

Julian Zuk

Branded

I thought freedom would feel like a rush of fresh air. Instead, it felt heavy, uncertain, and fragile. Every step I took outside the prison walls carried the weight of invisible eyes watching, waiting for me to trip. It didn't matter how many times I showed up responsibly, or how many months I stayed offense-free, the label of "felon" was louder than any and all of my actions. Fear followed me everywhere. Some of it made sense. After all, people want and need to feel safe. But much of it was exaggerated, built on stereotypes, driven by politicized assumptions, and fueled by disproportionate fear instead of facts. Criminologists call this "moral panic." To me, it feels like being reduced to my worst mistake, as if that's all I can ever be. It's exhausting to live constantly under the shadow of what others fear I might do.

Probation has made it explicitly clear that even one accusation—no matter how unfounded—could mean spending the rest of my life in federal prison. As a result, I can't do many things others take for granted, like enjoying a simple walk through my own neighborhood, because I must always anticipate the worst possible way my actions might be perceived. And yet, even under this constant surveillance, I find small ways to move forward —quiet acts of defiance against the idea that I am nothing more than my worst mistakes. By making these choices daily, I prove that I am more than their fear. But the weight I carried that day didn't begin at the prison gates, it began years earlier, with a single choice that would define me in ways that I never could have imagined.

The Weight of a Single Choice

I was eighteen when my life changed forever. One mistake, a decision made without a second thought, became frozen in time, casting me in stone, defining me not by who I would become, but by what I once did. What I did not understand at the time of my arrest was that I had just inherited a scarlet letter that wouldn't fade no matter how much time went by or what I did to make amends.

Even after serving my time, even after years of offense-free living, the world continues to see me through the lens of that single choice. I now know that prison gates don't open to true freedom. They crack open to a different kind of confinement, one I've come to call conditional freedom. This new world is governed by stigma, suspicion, and more than 44,000 laws and regulations that dictate where justice-impacted individuals may live, where they can work, who they are allowed to associate with, and in some cases, even whom we are allowed to love. It is a cage without physical bars, no less suffocating, no less controlling.

Since the day I committed my offense, I have stumbled, fallen, and eventually made the conscious choice to rise again. I've carried shame like a second skin, wrestled with despair, and clawed my way toward something that resembles healing. Over time, I've come to see my scars—not just as reminders of pain, but as maps. Maps not only for myself, but for others who may one day walk a similar path. This is the story of that journey: of pain and perseverance, of vulnerability forged into strength. And above all, it is a story rooted in hope, hope for a future where no one is defined by their worst mistakes alone.

Learning Vulnerability

For most of my life, I wore toughness like armor. Growing up, I was taught, directly and indirectly, that men don't cry, men don't talk about feelings, men don't admit weakness. The only emotion I ever recognized clearly was anger. Everything else, fear, shame, sadness, was buried until it showed itself as rage. It was in treatment that I started to break this pattern. I began to notice the small physical cues of my emotions: a headache that signaled frustration, the harsh self-talk of shame, the pacing that came with excitement.

Slowly, I learned to name these feelings before they became overwhelming. I practiced saying simple, awkward phrases: "I feel hurt." "I feel overwhelmed." Each time, it felt like ripping off armor I wasn't sure I could live without. But something unexpected happened: When I let myself be vulnerable, most people didn't reject me. They leaned in. They listened. They cared. For the first time, I began to build relationships based not on performance or bravado but on honesty. These emotionally intimate relationships with my peers in treatment became the foundation of my resilience. They taught me that vulnerability is not weakness. It is strength. It is the courage to be seen.

The Quiet Toll of Supervision

If stigma was one weight, supervision was another. At first glance, lifetime supervised release sounds like accountability, a second chance to prove yourself. However, for those of us who live under these policies, they feel like a suffocating cage, a reflection of society's deep-seated fear, misunderstanding, and hatred. Every layer of isolation, perpetual punishment, and stigma presses down on those already marginalized and demonized, designed to break us while hiding behind the unquestionable veil of public safety.

One of the harshest blows was being told I could not associate with other treatment graduates after graduation because they were all convicted felons. Thus, they were automatically seen as dangerous. These were the people who knew what it meant to wake up every day with the label, the fear, and the shame. More than anything, these were the human beings who could reach into the darkness with me, reminding me that I wasn't alone, refusing to let me forget what was at stake. Through their presence alone, as well as through their strength, they showed me that I could rise above what society expected of me and become something more. Yet I was told they were suddenly and arbitrarily off limits. I was mandated to cut ties with my strongest support, not because it made sense but because of a blanket rule and the minimal chance that somehow these relationships posed some sort of risk to the public and thus my probation officer's job security.

Falling and Rising Again

My journey has not been a straight line. Initially after my arrest I was unable and unwilling to accept responsibility for what I had done. I was selfish, immature. I blamed others. But I was also young, naïve. I felt scared and ashamed. I knew what I had done was wrong, but I didn't know how to take accountability or, more importantly, behave differently.

Consequently, I continued engaging in harmful behaviors that unfortunately hurt others. More recently, one morning when I felt particularly alone and isolated, I felt as though I was faced with the choice between engaging in unhealthy behavior (drinking to cope with my feelings) or engaging in behavior that was healthy but against the conditions of my release (reaching out to a treatment graduate).

After a lengthy conversation in my head, I made the unfortunate decision to drink. While, thankfully, nothing immediately problematic came of this decision, I realized that the thought process that led me to this decision was problematic and potentially dangerous. Both examples highlight the importance of viewing individual behavior in the context of personal circumstances and through a lens of grace.

While firm rules and boundaries are necessary, it is equally important to recognize when we may be expecting too much from others. We would never expect a young child to act as if they were a mature adult. Yet, we often expect people who have previously caused harm to behave as if they already have the skills to refrain from such behavior, even when we haven't taught them how, or provided an environment where those expectations are realistic.

To extend this analogy further, we all understand how difficult it is to give up lifelong habits, such as unhealthy eating, smoking, or drinking. And yet, this same level of grace and empathy is rarely extended to those struggling with harmful behaviors, poor impulse control, anger management issues, or mental health challenges. We wouldn't leave a child to navigate life alone, so why do we demand that those learning to overcome harmful behavior do so, and punish them when they inevitably fall short?

From Scar to Map: Giving Back

As I healed, I began to see my scars not merely as reminders of pain. They were maps, maps that could guide others walking through the same gates I once had. Just as older peers in treatment believed in me when I doubted myself, I now want to invest in those who are freshly released. I want to become a beacon of light for those stepping into freedom for the first time. I want to empathize with the crushing uncertainty of shame and the sense that the world is waiting for them to fail. I could tell them they are not alone, that they too can stumble and still rise. Most importantly, I would show them that their past does not have to define their whole story.

Mentorship is the bridge between empathy and action. It is not merely advice; it is presence. It is walking alongside someone when society has turned its back, bearing witness to their struggle and their courage. And yet, I am held back by a single choice I made over twelve years ago. Because of that choice, the government declares I will never be enough, that I will not be able to step into this role. Still, each time I extend a hand, I reclaim a little more of my own humanity. Giving back has become my way of attempting to make sense of this journey, of turning pain into purpose, of tracing a map through my scars for others to follow.

Reimagining Justice

Living under these conditions has given me a broader vision of justice, one that goes beyond punishment. To me, justice is not about perpetuating shame and fear; it is about transformation and accountability. It means seeing people, especially those who have harmed us, as more than their worst mistakes; creating meaningful pathways for healing, education, and contribution regardless of one's past; and ensuring that resources are equally available rather than withheld because of stigma, labels, or fear.

I have personally seen how fear-based systems fail both those who cause harm and those who have been harmed. Survivors are too often left with unanswered questions and no true healing. Offenders are reduced to threats rather than recognized as human beings who are not only capable of mistakes but also capable of tremendous change when given the proper tools and opportunities. Real justice must be transformative, addressing root causes, breaking cycles of violence, and offering rehabilitation that is genuine instead of symbolic.

When I look back on my journey, I see a life marked by mistakes but also by resilience. I see the weight of stigma, the suffocation of supervision, the heartbreak of setbacks. But I also see vulnerability turned into strength, persistence forged in fire, and scars transformed into maps for others, a reminder that no one should be seen as a single thing. Despite my mistakes, or perhaps because of them, I am majoring in transformative justice, a degree I have intentionally shaped so that my lived experience and formal education can together reimagine how justice-impacted individuals are treated.

The ultimate goal is to establish a peer-led organization that serves as a support network for those who have been negatively impacted by the justice system. By highlighting the lived experiences of those who have successfully reintegrated into society, I believe we can help break the cycles of abuse and mass incarceration that continue to plague our communities. Through this organization, I hope to empower both justice-impacted individuals and survivors, creating a space where healing, accountability, and rehabilitation are prioritized, ultimately contributing to a safer, more compassionate society for all.

Julian Zuk is a senior studying Transformative Justice whose academic work is shaped by his lived experiences navigating stigma, conditional freedom, and the possibilities of accountability and healing. His journey informs his commitment to reimagining justice through empathy, vulnerability, and community support.

The Moment That Lingers

Emily Perron

There is a photograph that sits on a shelf, its frame worn with age. In the picture, an old blue couch rests against the living room wall, and at the center my father sits with a soft smile tugging his lips upward. On his right, he holds a baby girl wrapped in white cotton, and on his left, I sit pressed against him, grinning at the camera. His large, steady arm is wrapped around me, pulling me close for the perfect shot. In that moment, it felt as if forever stretched ahead of us. Looking back now, I realize how short that forever truly was. It is my belief that every dream comes with the burden of difficulty, and my father faced more than his share. I did not understand it then, but as an adult I realize how admirable it was.

This captured moment is more than just a memory; it is a symbol of a loving father who spent time with his little girls. It represents who this man was to me. The details frozen in that photograph allow him to live on for an eternity we were never promised. His soft brown eyes twinkle with happiness, and his dark onyx hair, lightened by warm golden highlights for a touch of dimension, sweeps to the side in the comb-over I can still picture vividly. But a photo can only show so much. It doesn't capture the way he liked to sing along to songs on the radio while showering in the morning, or the way he played with mine and my siblings' earlobes in a strange but tender gesture of affection. It doesn't capture the long workdays, the classes he attended after his shifts, or the struggles he carried between those rare moments when he sat still long enough for a single picture.

When I think about my father, I remember the little things, the moments that became core memories etched deep in my heart. He had a way of turning routines into rituals. He always woke earlier than anyone else in the house to get ready for his day, and a melody would drift through the tiled bathroom walls into the surrounding rooms. Sometimes it was an old country tune, his mellow voice carrying the words to "The Chair" by George Strait, deep and soothing, a sound that somehow made the house feel safe. The faint smell of his cologne, Acqua di Giò, would mix with the steam from his shower, a clean, woodsy scent he chose carefully so it wouldn't give my mom a migraine. I can still hear his boots thudding down the hallway as he'd call out, "What's for dinner tonight?"

I often think about those mornings when I catch myself singing to fill the quiet, while driving my kids to appointments, cooking dinner, or cleaning around the house. Maybe it's something I inherited from him, because he was one of those people who sang everywhere: in the shower, in the car, even while working under a hood. Sometimes an old song we used to belt out together comes on, and I can't help but sing along, smiling through the lump in my throat.

It's funny how easily those songs bring back not just his voice, but everything about him, the way he looked when he came home from work, tired yet content. After a long day, the smell of diesel and oil clung to his clothes, something steady and familiar about him. He always wore his work jacket with his name, Mike, embroidered on the left side, the fabric stained and softened by years of labor. At night, he would stand at the sink and work a cherry blossom mechanic's hand scrub into his palms, gritty and sweet, chasing the grease from the lines of his skin. The clean notes never completely replaced the trace of the shop. It felt like both parts of him, the hardworking mechanic and the gentle father, coexisted in the air around him.

I remember sitting beside him on the living room couch, listening to his laugh spill out during comedies on the screen. His laugh filled the room, loud and contagious. And then there was his gentle habit of tugging on someone's earlobe, a gesture that felt strange at the time but is now missed more than I can say. These details may seem small, but together they paint the picture of a playful, loving parent. They are the moments that will endure, even long after any photograph has faded.

As vivid as his habits remain in my mind, they still feel close, like echoes that haven't faded. Even now, when I close my eyes, I can see him at our small kitchen table, the overhead light buzzing faintly as he flips through thick law textbooks. His hands are rough and scarred, still smelling faintly of motor oil as they move carefully over the pages. I can see myself sitting nearby, telling him a silly joke I heard at school while he studies, waiting for him to crack that simple smile that made everything feel light again. A soft fizz from his open Pepsi, his drink of choice when coffee isn't enough to keep him awake, drifts through the quiet. The image feels so clear, as if it could still be happening in the next room. I think about those nights whenever I'm up late working on school assignments, trying to finish what I started. That same drive to keep going, to push past exhaustion, feels like something he passed on to me. I want to succeed the way he tried to, to give my family the comfort and security he dreamed of for us.

Between those roles, he was still a friend, a brother, and most importantly, a father. On weekends, he liked to keep things simple: mowing the lawn in his worn cowboy boots, watching football, or playing video games with us. Our favorite thing to do together was play Guitar Hero and see who could get the highest score. He was always the winner, of course, because he had the unfair advantage of actually knowing how to play guitar. His laugh would echo through the house as he teased me for missing notes, and I'd pretend not to care, though really, I was determined to beat him one day.

When he wasn't home from the shop, he was working shifts at the Air Force Academy with my mom, the scent of popcorn and hotdogs still clinging faintly to him from the concession stands. Sundays were for family dinners, usually his homemade pizza or my mom's chicken parmesan. These weren't grand gestures, but they were the ones that mattered, the small acts of love that built our family's foundation. His ambitions weren't loud or boastful; they showed up in the sacrifices he made, in the way he pushed through exhaustion to study late into the night, and in the quiet hopes he placed on our shoulders.

In my own way, I try to do the same. I parent differently than he did, but I carry pieces of his love into the way I hold my kids close and the way I make time to laugh and be silly with them. He was a big cuddler, and maybe that's why I find comfort in those quiet moments of closeness now. To me, his dreams revealed a man who believed in perseverance, in the power of education, and in the promise of a brighter tomorrow.

His perseverance came with a price. Every dream he chased demanded more of him than most people realized. I didn't recognize it as a child, but now I understand how much strength it took for him to work long hours during the day and still attend night classes in pursuit of his degree. Having worked multiple jobs myself while taking classes and balancing family responsibilities, I can see now the toll those sacrifices must have taken on his physical and mental health.

What stands out most is how he never let those struggles show. He was always friendly to others, spending his downtime with the people who mattered most and putting on a brave face to hide the exhaustion I know must have felt overwhelming at times. Looking back, I see a man who carried heavy burdens yet still found the strength to move toward what he wanted, becoming the person he needed to be to raise his children in a loving home. I am proud to say that man was my father.

When I look at this photograph now, I see a man who wanted a brighter future than what we had in that moment. In the picture, we are frozen in a time that might not have been as simple as I believed, yet he made it feel that way. He left behind so much for us to carry forward. His quirky ways of showing affection, his deep belly laughs that filled a room, and his habit of singing through the house taught me that love often lives in the smallest gestures. His dreams, those long days of work followed by long nights of study, taught me the power of perseverance and the belief that education can open doors to a better life. Even his struggles, the ones he bore quietly with a brave face, remind me that resilience is not the absence of hardship but the determination to keep going despite it.

I keep that photograph within reach, and when I show it to people, I find myself smiling more than crying now. It reminds me that his love still lingers in the details of my life. And maybe one day, my children will have a photograph of us collecting dust on one of their shelves, and they too will reflect on the sacrifices a parent makes for the people they love.

Emily Perron is in her first year at Metro State University, studying Business Administration and minoring in Creative Writing. She is a dedicated book lover who enjoys quiet reading nights, fun creative moments, and time with her husband and their two small children.

The Internal Struggle:

Journal Excerpts from a Depressed and Anxious Young Adult in an Episode

Aimee Ilkka

No. 1

Feeling so stuck.
I have no desire to leave my bed.
I just sit rotting in it all day.
I doomscroll the day away on my phone
so I don't have time to think
about how unmotivated, sad, broken,
and fucking pathetic I feel.
Sometimes I wanna smash my phone with a hammer.
Our phones are the whole world now.
Everyone has one,
everyone uses one,
and I would be smashing my world.
I think I'm so attached because it gets me away from my own
thoughts.
Means I don't have to think about things
that make me uncomfortable and anxious.
Instead of facing it all,
I waste time on my phone, watching videos or TikTok,
scrolling through Instagram,
buying shit I don't need.
So how can I face the crippling thoughts?

No. 2

Why am I a nervous wreck?
Why am I scared to leave my house?
Do I realistically have anything to be afraid of?
No, I don't think so.
But there are people—too many people—
with intentions that aren't good or are downright evil.
Is that what I'm afraid of?
I see the worst in myself, so how could I ever see the best in
them?
It's difficult to leave my house.
No, it's difficult to leave my bed.
To go out into the world alone.
It's unbelievably anxiety inducing.
I break out into a cold sweat, get shaky,
can't control my racing thoughts.
There are too many people—
where do I stand?
And it all comes back to me, taking up my space as a human
in this world.
Why is that?
Is it because I don't believe I deserve it?
Why do I struggle so much to take up space in the world?
I'm forced inside, in solitude
that has made a monster of my mind,
trapped in an introspective whirlwind
of utter unworthiness.

No. 3

Recently, I've been sleeping more.
Sleep is truly the only time I feel at ease.
I look forward to sleeping and dread waking.

I wish I could sleep all the time,
but that's not an option,
unless I were to die.
I don't wanna die.
I just don't want to be going through this—
these moments.
I don't want to try to survive these painful moments.
Just get through.
Where is the light at the end of the tunnel they talk about?
I could use a light.
Every day is a struggle,
a battle with my life.
I feel so empty and purposeless.
I become so angry and irritated all the time because I'm miserable.
I'm so depressed and unmotivated.
All I do is lie in my bed
and wait until I can sleep again.

No. 3½

It's 11:23 and I wish I were asleep
But I'm staring at the ceiling
as tears come streaming down my cheeks,
and I wish that I could scream.
But is it only me, do you think of what could be?
In a day, a week, a decade … Will I find that missing piece?
And will I finally feel complete?

No. 4

I'm tired of myself, my mind, my issues, my mistakes.
But outwardly, my life is fine, so I just can't complain.
I'm trapped in my own mind, and I can't escape.
But I'll just pretend I'm fine

and live my life in pain.
There are only two people who do not experience painful
emotions.
First are psychopaths.
The second are dead.
It's inevitable, pain.
I've experienced a lot of pain this month, this year, in my life.
I believe that everything happens for a reason.
A child wrote me a card recently.
It said, don't let the bad times get the best of you.
It's true.
I have the power to make it through painful emotions
and difficult times.
I'm strong and resilient.
I grow through trials and become better.
It always turns out okay.
It's just a matter of how long that takes.
Until then,
I have to sit in the pain and discomfort
of not being okay.
Until it is once again okay.

No. 5

I can't keep my fucking plants alive.
I lay in my bed counting down the time until I can shut
my eyes.
I have dirty clothes I need to wash.
I haven't grocery shopped.
My gas tank is on empty,
mentally and physically.
But at least there's cotton candy skies,
and a thousand stars to light up the night.

There are lovers holding hands in an ice cream shop,
So I know that life is beautiful,
even when mine's not.

Aimee Ilkka is a Metropolitan State University student graduating in 2026 with a BA in Individualized Studies focused on art, psychology, and communications. She navigates multiple mental health challenges and uses her authentic voice to help others feel seen, heard, and validated.

I'm Sixteen

Dodi Vessels

I'm sixteen and stuck at home waiting for the phone call. I'm sixteen, on a Saturday, stuck at home, doing homework to kill the time. I'm sixteen when the phone rings. I get up, sliding my TV tray to the side, head into the kitchen, and pick up the phone attached to the wall. I'm sixteen and I spin the wired cord around my finger as you tell me to come pick you up.

I'm sixteen and on my way to a foreign road and a foreign house, following your directions. I'm sixteen when I pull into the driveway in Dad's car and see you stumble toward me. I'm sixteen and I love driving Dad's car. You both get in, Dad in the front and you, with help, get in the back seat. I'm sixteen when we pull out of that foreign driveway and leave the good times behind.

I'm sixteen when you are both arguing just before you throw up in the back seat. I'm sixteen when I pull over on the side of the road so Dad can clean you up. He puts you in the front seat and then refuses to get back in, he says he'll wait at the Subway across the street. I'm sixteen when I leave Dad, also drunk, on the side of the road and drive you the rest of the way home.

I'm sixteen when I finally pull into the driveway at home with you passed out in the passenger seat.

I'm sixteen when I struggle and fail to wake you up.

I'm sixteen when Sister comes home and helps me drag you inside.

I'm sixteen when I go outside and help clean up the vomit in Dad's car.

I'm sixteen when I pick up the corded phone and dial that Subway and they tell me

nobody is there.

I'm sixteen when I hang up the phone, worried, not sure what to do next.

I'm sixteen when the door finally opens, and Dad walks in. He walked all the way home

in his cowboy boots.

I'm sixteen when we never talk about that night again.

I'm sixteen when the sun rises and sets the next day.

I'm sixteen when one night becomes forever etched into my soul.

Dodi Vessels is a graphic designer, instructor, and storyteller who finds joy and inspiration in the quiet details of everyday life. When she isn't designing or teaching, she can be found exploring all things creative—painting, photography, drawing, and even a little gardening.

Sticks and Stones,

Broken Bones, & a Thousand Scars

Ximena Castillo Perez

When I look back now, I can still hear the sound of it all—
not the shouting, not even the crack of skin meeting skin—but
the silence that came after, heavy and awkward. The kind of
silence that sits in your bones. The kind that teaches you how to
disappear. As a child, I was taught that I was to be respectful to
my elders, but I now see that those lessons were meant to teach
me not to be defiant, because defiance was met with punishment.
No one outside ever asked questions. Children don't usually get
the language for the truth, and adults rarely want to hear it. So,
I learned to translate pain into politeness, to smile when people
said, "You're so mature for your age." They didn't know that
maturity was just the byproduct of fear—that wisdom had been
beaten into me.

When I was four or five, I accidentally became lost after
thinking that I had been left behind. I was found and brought
back to my family, and that's usually where movies just show
families filled with relief, but for me that was the beginning.
It was an aunt, whom now every family member that I have
communication with sort of hates, who decided she would teach
me what happened to children who abandoned their family. I
still remember the heat of poison ivy with each strike against my
legs, the sting of it against my skin, her voice cold and certain
that this was love disguised as a lesson. For years I told myself I
must have deserved it; after all I had walked away, right?

When I was around eight or nine, teachers began to notice
something. I'd get lost in daydreams, not turning in homework

and avoiding my classmates. They called it "behavioral issues." My mother took me to see a child therapist. The therapist asked me to draw my family. I wanted to draw what I saw—Mom and Dad working, older siblings who cared for me but still had a separate life that I did not want to engage in—but my parents told me what to put on the page.

"Draw everyone smiling," my mother said. "Make sure you're in the middle."

I drew what they told me. The therapist smiled politely, took notes, and sent us home with a label: "childhood trauma." No one said what to do with it. The diagnosis became another medical document in the pile, folded away like everything else.

There are pieces of my story that went missing for a long time. Suppressed memories, sealed off so tightly that even my dreams refused to touch them. When I was eleven, I think something finally broke in me—or rather, a series of some things—that made me carve physical scars in silence to cover the mental and emotional ones that were causing pain. I didn't remember them until I was twenty-four, sitting in therapy, when my mind finally unlocked the door it had kept bolted.

What surfaced wasn't a movie reel but fragments—flashes of confusion, betrayal, the unmistakable knowledge that someone had taken what was never theirs to take. I spent months doubting myself, wondering if remembering late made it less real. It didn't. The body remembers even when the mind doesn't want to.

By the time I was twelve, pain had learned how to change shape—no longer a hand from someone else, but a voice in my head whispering that I wasn't enough, that I was damaged, that I should take the punishment into my own hands. That year, I discovered the false relief of self-harm. It was control in a life where everything else was stolen. The first time my sister found out was the first time she looked at me like I was both fragile and foreign. I promised her I'd never do it again. I lied.

When I was fourteen, the darkness returned heavier. My second attempt was quieter, calculated, a test of whether the world would notice my absence. But I failed again, and I became an expert at concealment after that. Smiles, long sleeves, practiced laughter, pretend happiness. People think resilience means not breaking. But I learned that resilience is what happens after you break—the fragile, trembling choice to gather the pieces and carry them anyway.

There were teachers who suspected something but looked away. There were friends who asked questions I never answered. And there was me—hiding in plain sight, laughing too loudly, trying to become what they wanted me to be.

But trauma doesn't disappear just because you bury it under achievements. It seeps through. It whispers in your reflection, in your relationships, in the way you flinch when someone raises their voice too suddenly. It lingers in the corners of joy, reminding you it's never been entirely yours.

Adulthood came slow and steady—no big turning point, just a gradual realization that the child inside me was still crouched in a corner, waiting for the next blow. For years, I lived like that: functional but haunted. I built walls, called them boundaries. I called avoidance healing. The truth is, I didn't know how to live without the familiar ache of survival. Peace felt like foreign soil—soft, but unstable. When you've been shaped by pain, safety can feel suspicious. It took years before I began to unravel the knots. Before I learned that survival is not the same as living. That endurance, while noble, is only the first half of resilience. The second half—the harder one—is allowing yourself to heal.

Healing isn't cinematic. It's slow and unglamorous. It's crying in the employee bathroom because a customer's tone reminded you of something old. It's relearning how to accept kindness without scanning for the hidden cost. It's learning that love can be quiet, and that quiet doesn't always mean danger.

The turning point wasn't a single moment. It was a collection of small, stubborn ones. It was the day I said no and meant it. The day I looked in the mirror and saw not a victim but a survivor. The day I realized that scars, visible or not, aren't marks of shame—they're the proof that something tried to end me and didn't succeed.

Resilience, I've learned, isn't loud. It doesn't always roar. Sometimes it's the whisper that says, "Get up. Try again. One more time."

Recovery, for me, is an ongoing act of defiance I was taught not to make. It's choosing joy in a world that once taught me only fear. It's forgiving myself for the ways I survived when I didn't know better. It's rebuilding trust in my own body, in my own worth.

And slowly, art has returned to me—tentative at first, then defiant. I draw again now, not what I'm told to draw, but what I feel. My lines are messy, uneven, and honest. Each one is a small victory, a reclaiming of a language that was once taken from me.

Sometimes, I still hear echoes of the old voices. The ones that say I'm not enough, that I should've been tougher, quieter, better. But now, there's another voice that answers back. My own. It says: *You did enough. You were enough. You are enough.* And that voice—fragile, cracked, but still steady—is the truest sound of resilience I've ever known.

I once believed resilience meant armor, that strength was about never bending. But resilience is not about becoming unbreakable—it's about learning how to mend. It's about walking forward even when your knees shake, about showing up to life despite the ghosts that linger at the edges.

There are still nights when I wake up from dreams I can't quite explain. Still moments when my chest tightens at sudden noise. Still flashes of memory that come uninvited. But I no longer treat them as enemies. They're just reminders—that I've been through the worst and still found a way to live.

The world feels different now. Softer, but also wider. I notice things I used to miss: sunlight through leaves, laughter in crowded rooms, the quiet comfort of being safe in my own skin. I still carry tiredness in my bones—the kind that comes from years of fighting invisible battles. But it's kind of tiring now. The kind that comes after surviving the storm, looking out at the wreckage, and realizing that somehow, despite it all, you're still here.

The child in me thought resilience meant never crying again. The adult in me knows it means crying and still waking up the next morning.

Resilience is the sound of my own heartbeat, steady and defiant. It's the way I laugh now—freely, without flinching. It's the way I tell my story, not as a confession, but as a reclamation. Because this—these words, this truth, this voice—is mine. And after all the sticks, the stones, the broken bones, and the thousand scars, that's what they could never take from me.

Ximena Castillo Perez is set to graduate from Metro State in 2026 with a BA in Studio Arts and a minor in Creative Writing. They currently spend most of their time writing, painting, playing video games, and helping to manage their father's company in Minneapolis.

Academic Reentry as a Pathway to Belonging and Purpose

Andre Anderson

Academic reentry is a novel idea, an alternative to the traditional workforce pathway that returning citizens are often relegated to. The opportunity to join the academy after incarceration offers a newfound freedom to justice-impacted individuals like myself. Public land-grant universities have an obligation to serve all publics, regardless of background. This next step in my journey is an opportunity that was never afforded to me prior to prison. Reentry itself is a profound challenge for anyone making the leap back into society. Higher education is not a privilege; rather, it is a basic human right that must be offered to and supported for all. Justice-impacted individuals face many unique needs, from housing to transportation. These are second-order needs that often obscure the deeper necessities: belonging and purpose. A minimum-wage job cannot meet these fundamental human requirements. A collegiate pathway can.

A university is a community, and it functions as one. It provides agency, relation, and space: all requisites for a healthy life, if one chooses to engage. Within this community, belonging begins to form through each bond, connection, and interaction. For a returning citizen, this environment offers a safe place to let their guard down, to feel what true community can be, and in time, to develop purpose. This is where the pathway of reentry opens and a blue ocean of possibilities comes into view.

Academic reentry is not a service provision or a transactional handoff of goods. It is an invitation into the academy, extended from intuition and principle, without prerequisite, from day one. It represents one of the most promising possibilities for successful reentry, shifting the focus from avoiding reincarceration to fostering true integration and success. If our best measure of success is whether someone returns to prison within three years, we will never understand the problem, let alone imagine the solution. Yet in college, we are taught to do exactly that: to imagine solutions to complex problems.

Reclaiming my agency through education offers a vital alternative to the status quo: the mandate to take a minimum-wage job and "make it work." My future will not be foreclosed upon by this tone-deaf narrative. With each book I read, my ears are unstopped, and I begin to imagine the endless possibilities of my future as a justice-impacted student.

Andre Anderson is a graduate student at Metro State University in the Master of Advocacy and Political Leadership program. He serves as the Graduate Student Reentry Coordinator for the Transformation and Reentry through Education and Community (TREC) program and spends his free time distance running.

Coming To

Heather Young

The day I got sober wasn't really a day; it was more of a drawn-out series of unfortunate events that occurred over three days, or maybe four. It's hard to remember sometimes when it feels as though I've lived a dozen lifetimes since that final day. I hadn't been home in nearly three years. My addiction to both heroin and methamphetamine had completely taken over, and living on the streets had become normal. In the winter of 2017, I was living in a garage off West 7th Street in St. Paul. There was no insulation, and the only piece of furniture was a small brown ottoman, set a few inches off the concrete floor. The ottoman was old, dirty, and couldn't have been more than two feet by three feet long. I don't know where the ottoman came from, but I used it as a place to sleep on days when the exhaustion caught up with me. Somewhere along the line, I found three small space heaters to try and heat the giant two-car garage. Still, two space heaters weren't enough to make a difference, and plugging in all three would blow the circuit, causing the homeowner to react in a way that was possibly more violent than freezing to death. In my thirty years of life, I don't remember a Minnesota winter that it was ever as cold as it was that year, and every night when I would retreat to that garage, I secretly hoped that something would happen, and I wouldn't have to wake up and survive another day all over again. Looking back, my life was an ongoing suicide mission; I was barely living. I didn't care if I died, and truthfully, most days, I welcomed the idea.

A few days before my sobriety date, I had been out roaming the streets of St. Paul, trying to stay warm, and as the sun started to set, I made my way back to the garage. I walked around the house, down the long, icy sidewalk, and as I came to the garage, I noticed the door wasn't shut all the way. This wasn't a surprise to me because people were in and out of that garage every day, using it as cover for their nefarious activities. To them, it was nothing, but to me, those four walls were my only shelter. I approached the door and noticed that it wasn't just open; it had been broken into, and everything inside, except the ottoman, was gone. Small piles of garbage were left behind, some yard tools stood in the corner, but every piece of junk that I called mine had clearly been stolen, even the heaters. Feeling defeated, I sat on the ottoman, consumed all the heroin I had left, and blacked out.

How I made it this far in life is a complete miracle, because I couldn't tell you what happened next or how I ended up in a car with an old friend, but I do remember coming to—and she was not happy. The snow was coming down so fast that plows had not been through the residential streets we were on. She was frantic. She yelled about being out too late, wishing she had never picked me up, and that her mom would kill her if we ran out of gas in her car. Considering my state of incoherence, all of this was new information to me. I didn't know how I got into the car; all I knew for sure was that she was pissed and we needed gas. At this point in my life, I was accustomed to a criminal lifestyle, so I told her to go to the gas station, and I would take care of it. I had nothing to lose. Once we pulled in, she asked, "How are you going to pay for it?" I was honest: "Gas and go." Once again, she was frantic. She screeched, "You can't commit a crime in my mom's car!" I explained to her that if I were driving, the citation or criminal charge would fall on me, not her or her mom. She argued about it for a while but ultimately agreed. We switched spots as she slid into the passenger seat, and I started pumping the gas. As I was pumping the gas, she changed her mind and hopped back into the driver's seat. I sighed. My friend was not a criminal, let alone one to be trusted to drive away in a snowstorm after committing a crime. Not wanting to cause a scene any more than we already had, I told her in a stern tone that I needed to drive. Naturally, she refused, and as we left the gas station and pulled into a roundabout not more than three minutes down the street, the car was lit with blue and red lights. Unbeknownst to my friend, I had several felony warrants out for my arrest, and I was soon in the back of a squad car on my way to jail.

Addiction is a tricky thing. You think that at this point in the story, I'd admit defeat and just go.

Wrong.

Fearing the inevitable withdrawal, I thought up a plan. I told the officer that while he was running our names, I'd eaten all the drugs I had on me. Knowing a little bit about standard arrest protocol, I knew I would be taken to the hospital, where I would maybe have an opportunity to get high just one last time.

What I didn't account for was hospital protocol.

I was transported to Hennepin County Medical Center, where I woke up sometime the next day, quite groggy. I had a heart monitor attached to me, an IV in my arm, and those ugly slipper socks wrapped around my feet. Sitting up in the hospital bed, I felt frail. I hadn't been eating regularly, and with each movement, I could feel the IV line digging around in my skinny little arm. I stood up, clearly under the influence of something foreign to me. As I opened the door and peeked outside, I saw no one. Not a police officer, not a nurse, nobody. So I fled. I detached the IV line, leaving the port in my arm. I unhooked all the heart monitor wires, dug my clothes out of the plastic, electric-blue property bag, and left.

I made my way to the downtown library, as if I hadn't just escaped a felony arrest, and I called a different friend to pick me up, one I thought was a better driver. I got in the back of a busted-up Buick, asked for a cigarette, and drifted off. I was in and out of it for most of that day. Sometime after the sun had set, I started to come around, and I remember waking up, still in the backseat, unmoved, wondering if we had been in the car all day. The driver was a stranger to me, but somewhere in the conversation, he assured me that I would feel better soon, but we never made it.

Shortly after the driver made this declaration, the car behind us lit up with sirens, and my heart stopped—this time, it was different. As soon as the lights swirled, the car was full of chaos. I could feel it. The guys were yelling at each other, swearing every curse word under the sun, and panicking about the drugs they had in the car. As they looked to me, I knew it was on me to take care of the drugs, and without a second thought, I ate all of them.

The police swarmed the vehicle. I was cuffed and loaded into the back of a St. Louis Park squad car, where I proceeded to give the officers a false name. I identified myself as Carrie. I sat there for a while, waiting for a female officer to arrive and search me. As I sat there, cuffed in the backseat, everything started to fade out until I heard the door open. Feeling extremely ill, I didn't look up. All I heard was a woman say, "Her name isn't Carrie." She knew who I was. Somewhere in the haze, the voice sounded familiar. I turned my head to the side and realized God had sent an angel to stop my complete self-destruction. The woman was a friend from high school. She was someone who had known me before drugs were ever a problem, and on this night, she would be the person who would save my life.

She pulled me out of the squad car, searched me, pulled me in for a hug, and said, "It's time to go." She wasn't harsh, she wasn't cold, and I knew as soon as she identified me the gig was up. She helped me back into the squad car and sent me on my way. The officer started the engine and said, "You've been on quite the run." Feeling very sick, I knew something wasn't right, and I began to seize. I remember the officer asking me what I had taken. I don't know if I answered him or not, but I remember the flashlight he shone in my eyes, and then once again, everything was dark.

December 20, 2017, I woke up in North Memorial Hospital. I knew the date because it was written on the whiteboard at the end of my hospital bed. I was groggy, I was sick, and the sharp pain of despair had settled deep into my bones. I shuffled to the door only to find it locked. I knocked on the window from inside, feeling like a caged animal, but nobody came. I didn't even try knocking twice. I sat on the floor and started to cry. I didn't need anyone to explain why the door was locked; I already knew. I was a danger to myself. I was out of control.

After a couple of days in the hospital, I finally stabilized. Poisoning by methamphetamine was the final diagnosis, but I was monitored for potential cardiac arrest in the psychiatric ward due to my mental and emotional instability. The nurses were kind, and perhaps I was sensitive, but I felt a sense of pity when they came in to talk to me, handling me like I was fragile.

I was taken into custody from that hospital room and transported to Hennepin County jail. The withdrawal was as bad as I had anticipated. Compounded by the recent poisoning, for nearly a week, I couldn't eat. Another inmate helped me shower and comb my hair when I couldn't lift my arms above my head; I was a wreck. Every day I spent in jail this last time was brutal. My body hurt, my skin crawled, and I sobbed for days on end. I remember the feeling of utter defeat. I was almost successful in ending my life, and then I learned that God had another plan.

I was released a few weeks later to an inpatient treatment program and then referred to a long-term program to address my behaviors. This wasn't unusual. I had been booked and released to treatment countless times before this trip, but this last time, I stayed. Every time I thought about running from treatment, I thought of that garage. I thought about all the tears I had cried in there, and how many times I hadn't felt safe, and with each new day, I made a conscious decision to stay. One day led to another, and things started to get better. It wasn't always easy, and some days are messy, but in the end, I've made it, I'm sober, I'm happy, and life is beyond beautiful.

Heather Young is in her first year at Metro State, pursuing a degree in Human Services Leadership and Administration. She is a person in long-term recovery who aims to inspire others on similar paths, creating safe spaces where struggles are acknowledged without judgment.

The Walk for Water

Justin Shukuru

There is always something about water that makes me remember. Water keeps my memory honest.

The roof wakes first. The plastic sheeting over our rafters lifts with the wind and settles with the cold. It never stops working. Inside the dim, almost-morning, the clay-and-wood walls hold the night's cool like a pot holds water. I lie still and listen the way Mama taught me to listen. I sort the air for useful truths. No rain, so the path will be dusty. A light wind, so the smoke from cookfires will travel and not fold back into people's lungs. Voices are far for now. If we move quickly, we can find the line before the line becomes an argument.

Confiance, my brother, is already up. I hear the soft scrape of rope against plastic as he unties the jerrycans we anchor at night so they do not walk away on their own. Those yellow bodies click together like teeth in a tin mouth. We do not waste breath on greetings. Our bodies have been holding this conversation for years. If he stands, I stand. If I reach for a handle, he is already reaching for the other.

The jerrycan handles are thin, the kind that bites into your hands before you even leave the yard. They were meant for adults, not boys with wrists like broomsticks. But we never say that out loud. Saying it doesn't make the walk shorter.

Outside, the air is cooler, sharper. It carries the dry taste of dust and the faint sweetness of morning smoke. We join the others already on the path, a small army of yellow containers and bare feet. The rhythm of sandals slapping the earth becomes a kind of music, soft, steady, necessary. Every step is an agreement: we go, we return, we endure.

The path winds through the scrub, past tents and the ghosts of old fires. We walk in silence except for the creak of the rope handles. Some carry jerrycans on their heads, others drag them by the neck like stubborn dogs. I count distance by landmarks: the bent tree, the rock shaped like a chair, the split in the road where the older boys sometimes talk about things they'll never see.

The ground remembers every dry season. The cracks hold the shape of feet from years before. When I was smaller, I used to think if I stepped in the same prints, the walk would hurt less. It didn't. The earth doesn't keep promises. It only keeps score.

When the sun rises, it rises fast. Shadows vanish like secrets. Sweat comes before thirst. I bite the inside of my cheek to distract myself from how long the road still is. The jerrycan bangs against my leg like a reminder; every drop we carry must be earned.

At the water site, the line is already long. We set the jerrycans down in a row, claiming our place. Dust lifts from the ground and clings to our skin, mixing with sweat until we're painted the same color as the earth. The women talk in low voices, sometimes arguing, sometimes laughing. The younger kids sit in small circles, tracing shapes in the dirt with sticks. No one wastes energy on standing tall. We all know that waiting is another form of work.

When it's finally our turn, the water hits the jerrycan's mouth with a hollow sound. Clear, cold, alive. I dip my fingers in and let the chill move up my arm. For a moment, everything feels possible. We seal the caps and tie them together with rope. The return walk is heavier, slower. Every step pulls the world downward. My shoulders burn. My hands ache. But I don't let go.

Halfway home, my brother slips. The jerrycan tips, spills a mouthful of water into the dirt.

We both freeze. The water disappears instantly, leaving only dark soil where it touched. I look at him, and he looks at me. No words. Just the shared understanding that what's lost won't come back. He grips the handle tighter, and we keep walking.

By the time we reach home, the sun is high. Mama is waiting at the door, her hands on her hips, her face half-worry, half-pride. She doesn't ask if we struggled. She already knows. She takes the jerrycan, opens it, looks inside, and says one word that means everything: "Mwakoze." Thank you.

The rest of the day moves slowly. My arms feel like stones. But every time I lift the cup to drink, I think of the road, the dust, the spill, the sound of water hitting plastic. I think of how even a small loss can feel like a wound. And how we walk anyway.

Years later, when I wait for other things, a shipment, a degree, a call that decides a future, I still feel that same rhythm. The ache that becomes endurance. The thirst that teaches patience. The way water taught me what strength sounds like: quiet, heavy, moving forward.

Justin Shukuru is a junior in Metro State's BS plus MBA program. Born in Congo and raised in a refugee camp, he rebuilt his life in Minnesota and now writes about survival, belonging, and starting over; his memoir, I Wasn't Invited, I Showed Up Anyway, *came out in 2025.*

A Hmong Thing

Michael Vang

It's 1999. Mom and Dad are at work. They drop me off at my friend Sean's house. Sean is my nephew, and even though he is older than me, because his mom is my oldest sister, I am his uncle. I am seven. He is eight. The white kids at school always tell me that it is weird. I tell them that it is just a Hmong thing.

Sean lives at his grandma's house. They aren't Christian like we are. His grandma always has these sticks burning, and her house always smells like old people. Our house doesn't smell like that. I tell myself it must be a Shaman thing.

When we sit down to eat, I look down at my bowl of boiled pork and rice. I like boiled pork and rice. But even if I don't, I know not to complain. After we are done, Sean takes me up to a bedroom. On the wall there is a rope that is tied into a larger hoop. It looks like the one he wears around his wrist.

"What is that?" I ask, because it isn't a cross like we have at my house.

"There's a ghost there," Sean says. "It holds a ghost. Don't touch the string, or the ghost will be able to follow you home." His words scare me. I don't want a ghost following me home.

"But you can touch the wall, right? It's the string that you can't touch," I said.

"Yeah," Sean places his hand in the middle of the loop, touching the wall. "You'll be good as long as you don't touch the string."

I feel a need to show off how brave I am to my friend. I reach out and put my head in the middle of the circle of string. I pull away faster than I like to admit. But we laugh, then go outside to play.

And as we kick a soccer ball around a yard covered in leaves, I think back to the string.

Did I touch the string on accident? Sean is kicking around the ball, but I see someone also running beside him.

I see a ghost. I touched the string, didn't I? But the ghost does not do anything to hurt us. It only runs beside Sean. It does not kick the soccer ball; it does not trip him. Even when Sean goes to play with his younger brother Troy, the ghost comes up next to me, and I put my arm around him like I have known him forever. He's my friend too.

And he's coming home with me.

When my mom and dad come to pick me up, I get in the car and wave goodbye to Sean. I keep my arm around my new ghost friend. He will follow me home.

"Dad, are ghosts real?" I ask.

"We don't believe in that," Dad answers.

"We believe in God," Mom says.

"Okay." I sit back. I know better than to ask questions.

I listen. I don't ask questions.

I guess believing in God means we don't believe in ghosts.

My arm falls back to my side.

My ghost friend is gone.

It must be a Chrisian thing.

*****

I couldn't have known that this memory would be one of the last with my best friend. My family moved out of St. Paul and into the suburbs that year. At the time, we were one of the only families out there. I stood where our finished house was, and looking down at the intersection of our street, I saw that the other houses were just stacks of wood and piles of dirt. We were one of the only houses that was finished, and we were, for sure, the only Hmong family in the neighborhood. I learned how to read and speak English better. But I was still embarrassed every time Mom and I arrived to school late. I would dive behind a counter in my second-grade classroom to avoid being seen, only to be reprimanded by my teacher, looking down at me through her glasses that sat on her nose. Being the only Hmong kid in that class, it felt like being consistently late was a Hmong thing.

I wouldn't see another Hmong person around my age for five years. In 2004, at thirteen, I met David. And even though I had never met him before our first-period gym class in seventh grade, all of the white kids asked us if we were brothers or if we were related because we had the same last name.

"Probably. Somewhere down in our family tree," I said. I don't even know if it was true. But at the time, I guessed that it was a Hmong thing.

*****

When 2006 came around, I was in high school. My neighborhood had been filled up with people; the stacks of wood and piles of dirt had turned into suburban-style houses that all looked like the same blueprint with different-colored wall panels and roof tiles. But my family was still the only Hmong family.

After seven years of not speaking a full sentence in Hmong, I had noticed something: I lost my accent and my ability to pronounce words. My tongue wouldn't roll with the tone of the words I wanted to say the way it used to when I was speaking the language like a master at five years old. As a matter of fact, I couldn't count to ten, only to five. This was when fate, the universe, God, whatever it is by its many names played a joke on me. In high school, for the first time since 1999, I saw more Hmong people than ever before. Before, it was me and David in junior high. In high school, there was Chao, Bruce, Brent, Katherina, Mihoko, Peter, and so many others I never got to know. But in those seven years, I had lost my language, and my demeanor—I had lost my identity.

I didn't know how to act when I was around them. I didn't use slang, I didn't sag my pants, I didn't gel my hair, and I didn't speak Hmong. I didn't have the same culture they did. What they emulated was something that Hmong people did to find an identity in a country where they have none. They are, after all, Hmong people.

The identity they emulated had been taken out of me—either lost to time or taught away because of the environment I was put in at a young age.

I can never be a white person, but I grew up in an environment with only white people, and that is what I emulated. Among this new group of Hmong people, I didn't belong. I can say that "it's a Hmong thing" to deal with lost identity and identity confusion. After all, I am Hmong.

But the thing is, it doesn't feel like I am.

But … that's a Hmong thing, too … isn't it?

Michael Yer Vang is a senior at Metro State who plans to graduate with a double major in English and Ccreative Writing in the summer of 2026. When not studying, he spends his time at home reading, wondering, writing, and trying to figure out what to do next.

Plunging from That Cocoon

Russell Melby

As a kid, I'd often run away.

I.

I was a hearing child with Deaf parents (a CODA, or "Child of Deaf Adults"), raised strictly Pentecostal, yet to be diagnosed with being on the autism spectrum. In my head, I was set apart from everyone, a sort of outcast, mostly because of the ways I'd obsess over little things. I was an elementary schooler, and I read a lot of books other kids my age didn't read. *Lord of the Rings* and H.G. Wells were particular favorites of mine, along with Captain Underpants, but I couldn't share this love with anyone but myself—not when most kids preferred to talk about Bionicle or Star Wars. This sense of loneliness would often mutate into a sort of buttheadedness, and I'd argue with my parents often. I'd want to escape, to disappear. My siblings weren't much help with that either.

It's funny, but I don't really remember the content of those fights with Mom and Dad. After some aggressive signing in ASL, I'd say something in declaration like, "None of you understand me. I'll show you. I'm leaving!" and I'd stomp away with my little feet through the front door. In those moments I truly felt like I was forging a path for myself away from my parents and siblings. I relished the fear and excitement of venturing out on my own, as well as the twisted feeling of wanting to prove my point. The kids in C.S. Lewis's *Chronicles of Narnia* series, after all, seemed to do alright for themselves when they ventured out through that magical wardrobe into an enchanted land. I remember those nights my heart would beat hard in my chest as I'd walk through the dark streets, where scary men or witches would prowl behind the corners of my mind.

I only ever got as far as the next two streets before spinning around and heading back home. It turned out the world wasn't as magical as I thought.

II.

A lot of people may recall hating homework. I must've been allergic to it. Those sheets we'd take home to write in, whether it was for English or history, were torture. They made my skin itchy and my legs restless.

"Have you done all your homework?" my mom would sign to me.

"No, and I'm not going to," I'd say, and I'd kick and scream verbally. Mom would sometimes have to drag me to the dinner table to do my work. This led to plenty of fights between us. In our household, Mom was the queen when it came to school. Mom was the one who had graduated college, and naturally she felt school was important. I, on the other hand, felt it was a bore. I wanted to watch *Veggie Tales*, not do fractions.

One night, while my face was hot with tears, I wanted Mom and Dad to think I actually ran away. I must've been particularly pissed off then. It's strange to think I got such a thrill on the idea of putting my parents through the stress of losing a child.

I crawled into the back of the family Chrysler, nuzzling into a pile of blankets. I hid in there for maybe half an hour—maybe more. After a while, my mom must've gotten worried, because I heard her as she got into the van and started to drive around, most likely looking for me. It was fun bumping around in the back as the van veered left and right, but it didn't take long for the guilt to creep into my heart. Despite the fights, I really admired Mom, and I felt dirty and lonely where I was.

I tapped her on the shoulder to get her attention. "I'm back here," I signed, and I apologized.

The look of relief she gave me, the way her dark eyes brightened at the sight of me, was enough to show that, despite our differences, she really cared for me. Not many kids can say that.

III.

A rocket made of cardboard sat in my room, ready to take me away. Gleaming pieces of duct tape held it together. There was a little window with a layer of plastic wrap to peer through. The rocket stood as a piece of comfort in the back of my mind in times I wanted to leave, those times my siblings really pressed my buttons. I'd built it myself, with my own hands. I'd first read Frank Asch's *Star Jumper: Journal of a Cardboard Genius* in the fifth grade. After that, something just clicked for me. The story followed a kid who hated his little brother. The kid happened to be a brilliant inventor, using cardboard and things he'd find on the street to build a rocket so he could escape the Earth. I related to this. My brother and sister, both younger than me, knew the right words to tear me to shreds. We rubbed each other the wrong way, with my developmental disability becoming more and more apparent to everyone but myself.

Later that same year, we had a kid in class who happened to have Asperger's syndrome. We had to watch a video in class all about it. At the time, little things seemed familiar to me in that video, though I didn't yet know why.

I never flew away in that rocket.

IV.

My main form of escape, as I got older, was my bedroom. That was where all my treasures were. I'd sit in there like a dragon on his heap, just proudly wasting away. That was where I'd paint on my canvases to take out my anger, mostly abstract or splatter stuff while blaring The Beatles on my Kindle Fire. Other times I'd wail away as I strummed my Jay Turser acoustic guitar, much to the annoyance of my sister, who happened to be my next-door neighbor. I'd also watch shows on my phone by slipping it in a little pocket above me in our bunk bed. (I used to share the room with my brother, until he wanted his own independence and started sleeping upstairs in the living room.) High school was rough. Relationships were rougher. Friends were hard to come by, but there were those special few, people I met in chess club as well as the anime and gaming club. The dating game, on the other hand, was not in my favor.

"I'm tired of this. You are so fucking annoying," someone responded as I struggled to understand the need for space in relationships.

Identities vied for the spotlight at that time. Was I merely Autistic, a CODA, or perhaps a misunderstood genius? My head was perhaps the largest it had ever been in those days. Copernicus was mistaken; I was the center of everything.

When I got a TV in my room, I'd use it to watch movies and anime. I remember the first time I rented *Dune* (1984), for example, and how I'd compare the scenes with Frank Herbert's book, which I'd just read. There was also the time I rented Cronenberg's remake of *The Fly*, and I relished every gory minute as my stomach would churn at Jeff Goldblum's transformation. My room was another dimension for me. My own TARDIS. A no-space where I could get away mend examine myself. It felt safe to lie on my bed and let my eyes wander the bookshelves, my vinyl collection, and my assortment of action figures. My own cloud nine, my room shielded me from the pains of the outside world.

I had yet to leave my parents' house and begin the real change. But in those moments, I'd still think, "This'll do."

R.J. Melby is in his first year at Metro State. When he is not writing memoir, he likes to dabble in science fiction, horror, and songwriting.

Elementary Education

Paula Foreman

When I say Grayson throws himself into reading, I am not speaking metaphorically. It's a rare day that the chairs at my desk remain on their feet after he crash lands into my tutoring space. He goofs around with a sticker and the decision about where to affix it. On the wall, his shirt, or his eyelids, anywhere except his daily attendance chart, which is the reason stickers exist here. I wait through his shenanigans without comment, a move that he mistakes for patience. Tossing the stickers aside, he flops onto the table, today's reading passage pinned between his forearms, and beetle-eyes it like a crime investigator. He counts down "Three-two-one." I click the one-minute timer, and he reads, voice raised, because in Grayson Land, volume and speed are one and the same. The timer beeps as he reads the 110th word of the passage. On the next try he gets to 122 words in a minute, and tops out a third reading at 132. This practice is important, as it simulates the progress monitoring we do each week. Those scores indicate that Grayson is at last reading at grade level, well ahead of the forty-six words he mustered when we began together. He loves it.

And then there's Nila. A page of three-letter, short A words wait on my desk next to a sound awareness exercise (which we tutors refer to as a game). Nila stops fiddling with my timer, flumps sideways in her chair, and digs in her heels. She jams her purple Crocs into the carpet and scrapes her chair backward into the hall, away from me and the offending exercises. Um, games. Her beaded braids swing around her face in refusal.

"I am not doing that."

Ignoring her, I slide the page between us and sound out the first letters, hoping she'll play along.

"Your turn," I prompt. "No," she insists. "I'm not doing that either." I concede. "OK, we'll start with the game. Let's blend two words to make a new word. Book. Mark. Bookmark." Her angry hand slams the table. "I SAID I'm NOT doing it!" Kids don't learn from people they don't like.

Right now, Nila's stony stink-eye and scowly pout telegraph how much she intends to learn from me.

One effective tutoring strategy is to offer choices. We start small. Bluey stickers or Batman? "Bluey." Fine. I hand Nila the sticker sheet and return the rest to the supply tray. "No WAIT!" she demands. Her favorite phrase. Girl can't decide anything without Nowait. It's time to put the markers away. Nowait. Your teacher's expecting you. Nowait. Nila, that's the fire alarm. Nowait. Her eternally snotty nose and indifference to the use of Kleenex are the source of my third eye infection in two months. Daily, I issue reminders to stop grabbing flashcards-paper-pencil-markers from my hands. A specialist who also works with her calls her a leader. Sure, why not.

Today I can think of another word, but it's not permitted in school.

Prior to having my own, I didn't love kids, at least not in the abstract, though there were specific children that were very likable. My two sons, for example, though I wasn't wild about them during labor. Even as an opinionated two-year-old, I considered my infant brother hopelessly uninteresting. I used to think that people who claimed to just love children simply didn't have them.

But for all of their squirreliness, it's easier for me to deal with eight-year-olds than grownups. Maybe that's because my taste isn't that far off from an eight-year-old's. And mostly, I like how kids' unvarnished perspectives reveal how cool I'm not, even when I pretend I am. A week after my dog died, I dragged my weepy self back to school and tried to act all I'm fine. My first student of the day wasn't fooled. This is a kid whose name I often hear his teacher snap in exasperation, as in: Jer-e-MY-ah! He sized me up in one look. "Are you sad?" My first impulse was of course to lie through my teeth and assure him things were fine. Just fine, and thanks for asking. Except it's really hard to lie to someone who counts on hearing you tell the truth that you think you're protecting them from.

"Yes. I'm sad," I admitted. "But I feel better because you asked."

This is also the kid who calls me bruh when I misplay my cards in our weekly UNO card games. I am so not a bruh, but I love how the word enfolds me into his circle of belonging. In the way of sturdy relationships, we occasionally lock horns. One day he greeted me with, "Will you tell me how old you are?" Sorry, but no. And he persisted, begging and whining, nearing one of his famous meltdowns that sometimes call for a visit from the school behavioral specialist.

"This is the thing," I began. "The answer to your question is yes or no. I chose no. If you want people to take you seriously, accept their answer." His widened eyes revealed his surprise that I took him seriously enough to explain. We both learned something about the importance of setting limits.

At home and with no one who needs me to set a good example, I'm sometimes known to rave at the coffeemaker and blame my car keys for walking out on their own. With my young charges, I become more the person I wish to be, patient and forgiving, trying day after day to make our relationships work. Thanks to them, I sometimes succeed. They are my better angels, even when they're not.

Paula Foreman has been writing since she could hold a pencil. She lives in St. Paul with her husband, who helps her farm, and her border collie, Cedar, who doesn't.

Woman and Freedom: A Memoir

Hanah Renstrom

As a young girl I never dreamed of college; no one in my family had ever talked about it. It seemed like a distant dream that only other kids might get to experience. When we started college tours in my junior year of high school, I remember going with friends knowing that they were looking with intent. I was looking to see what it was like with no real conviction that it would be a part of my reality. I didn't think I would ever be able to afford it, nor were my grades good enough to get in. I never really felt smart, but I knew I wasn't dumb either. I didn't know what to think about my future, but I knew I didn't want to be poor anymore. It's exhausting being at the mercy of other people's generosity.

My dad left when I was five, my mom got a job out of necessity, her dreams of being a stay-at-home mom ripped from under her. Into the workforce she went with little experience, or desire; she got a job at a tobacco shop down the road. It seems the dreams we had and the cards we were given were never able to line up just right. I loved going to work with her, though. My younger brother and I would hang out in the cigar room; I can still smell the smoky sweet smell of the cedar. Although our family was small, the five of us had enough love that it never felt void. My mother's parents were always there to pick us up from school, and we would stop at either Wendy's or McDonalds, and Burger King on the weekends when we'd go grocery shopping. My brother and I would squeeze into the front seat between my grandparents until we got too big and had to sit in the back of my grandpa's GMC covered pickup, Big Red. My brother and I would play the statue game whenever we rolled past a cop.

They lived thirty minutes north of our apartment on a lake that became a safe haven for us. Our grandmother's eyes were glued to us like a hawk whenever my brother and I were out in the lake. My grandparents believed in us. My grandpa used to tell me that I could be president, and my grandma used to tell me I could be a movie star. The values at the time were different, but I knew they really meant it.

My grades as a kid were good. It wasn't until freshman year of high school that they took a turn. I remember sitting in my ninth-grade algebra class looking at a GPA of 1.69 and feeling true shame. After a meeting with an advisor, I knew something had to change. I was able to get my GPA into the 2.0 range by junior year. Everyone was talking about where they were applying to. I applied to one college, and it was the community college in town. I remembered asking myself why I would go to an expensive college when I didn't even know what I wanted to do. Then one day, I was praying and asking God to give me some direction. "What do you want me to do?" I asked, as I was leaving Bill's Superette gas station. I felt in my spirit that I was going to be a nurse. I originally rejected the idea, because my grandmother on my father's side was a nurse and she was a less-than-admirable person. But I have always trusted the Lord since I was a little girl. I knew that he had a plan for my life, despite the chaos around me I knew that he would protect me and point me in the right direction. I started taking classes at the local community college. I started with a psychology class. I was shocked when I not only passed but got an A. My next class I took was communications, and that was when every-thing changed. I remember questioning everything that I was doing; I wanted to do everything right. I asked to meet with my professor to discuss an upcoming assignment to make sure I was on track. I remember at one point in the conversation he looked at me and said to me, "You are very bright." I never had heard that from a teacher before, and that little seed of encouragement took root in my heart and I began to believe it. I almost cried leaving the meeting because this was a man I truly respected. He carried himself with such reverence, and I knew he meant what he said. I carried that belief all the way through my generals and into nursing school.

My last year of nursing school, 2021, was the most difficult year of my life. I was in a toxic relationship with a close friend who was narcissistic, and the time I should have been studying was spent planning her bachelorette party. This friend and I had only rekindled our relationship a few months prior to her asking me to be in her wedding. I wrestled with the idea, and against my better judgement, and my boyfriend's plea, I agreed.

It was the week before the last week of nursing school finals in my final semester, and instead of locking myself into a study vault, I was buying small party favors on Amazon and ordering custom cupcakes. Racking up credit card debt and stress, I held on to the hope that it was going to be over soon, and at least my friend was going to be happy. Except, that was far from the truth.

The day of the party came. I barely slept that night. I had spent all day decorating and curating this perfectly executed party only to be ignored by the bride all night. I continued to push through the night, checking up on people, making sure the rental house was cleaned up to make sure that the bride got to enjoy her time. The gifts were the moment I broke. When she opened the gift I got her, which contained a bottle of expensive tequila, custom slippers, and other personalized items probably totaling around $400, she barely batted an eye or gave a sincere thank you. I was done. I remember thinking that nobody is going to help me get the future I need to and it was time to focus on myself. No more people-pleasing. Nobody was going to pass my courses for me, and if I ever wanted to crawl my way out of poverty, I needed to stop putting everyone else but myself first.

When the week of finals came, I was studying and just barely passing my courses. I had one test left. It was the hardest one yet, and if you know anything about nursing school grades, you know that the grading scale is skewed. Anything below a 78% is failing. I needed at least 78 points to pass; otherwise I would have to take the course all over again.

I got a phone call. It was my mom.

My grandmother, Sheryl, had passed away from brain cancer. I thought we had more time; it went so fast. I wanted her to see me become a nurse, to be proud of me. I wanted to be able to tell her I did it. But that time was gone. To make it all worse, family has a complicated history with my mother's older sister. She was coming into town from Florida, and I knew my mom didn't want to be alone with her. It's her story to tell, but let's just say it was warranted.

I had a choice: keep studying for my last final, or stop every-thing to be with my grieving mother. I chose family, said a prayer to God, and I felt his grace that he would help me through.

After visiting with my mom, I came back that night with plans to take the final in the morning. I was exhausted, every-thing in me was drained, I was breaking down, and I had a migraine in the middle of my final that made me vomit. After I cleaned myself up, I went back to the computer and finished the test; after all, the show must go on. It was done. When you grow up in survival mode, a career, a degree is more than just that, it's your livelihood. My boyfriend at the time, who is now my husband, was supporting us in hopes that one day we would be able to travel, to have a life and a family and not live in constant stress.

Then I waited. Over the next week while we waited for the test results, I went through waves of acceptance and utter despair. My friendships were crumbling, my family was shrinking, my dreams were within arm's reach, but still there was so much unknown. I was out of control. I went from praising God one moment to smoking a cigarette the next. I remember grabbing one of my boyfriend's Marlboro menthols and sneaking outside to sit in his 2006 Honda Pilot. I sat there in silence, and as I smoked, I also prayed. I told God I couldn't take it anymore. I just couldn't handle the weight of my future. And if he really gave me that dream junior year of high school, then he needed to help it become a reality. My identity was no longer in being a nurse or a successful person. I was worthy despite that. I was worthy when I had a GPA of 1.69, and I was just as worthy now. I remember after this cathartic experience it felt like a huge weight had been lifted off my chest. I remember repeating a song by Maverick City Music titled "Wait On You" in my living room and just dancing and praising the Lord for a hope in things I couldn't yet see. I decided that I would wait on the Lord and accept whatever outcome he had for me.

So the day came. My nursing school group chat was flooded with texts saying the results were in. My heart started to flutter and simultaneously sink into my stomach. I pulled up D2L on the computer and sat there for a minute before finally clicking into the results. I had scored a 78 out of 100. No more, no less, exactly what I needed to pass. This moment I will never forget.

I cried knowing that nothing was an accident. God gave me exactly what I needed in that moment so that I would remember that it was not my strength. It was intentional. It was exact. Just like God.

Years later I walk through my workplace as an RN at the best hospital in the country while giving my mom a tour. As we admire a large bronze statue titled "Man and Freedom," we both tear up thinking about how proud my grandparents would have been to see where I am now. They are both gone now, but the lessons I learned I will pass down. It's not necessarily a story of resilience or grit in the traditional sense, but more of weakness and surrender. The thing is, I am not that strong. I am quite fragile. Some days I still feel inadequate, some days I don't, but it's not about feeling. It is about having faith in something greater than ourselves. It's easy when you've overcome a lot of adversity in life to become prideful, to look back and say, "Look at what I did." I try not to think that way, not in a sense of false humility, but truly acknowledging that there were many key players who have a role in my story. I didn't manifest my dreams; I have been blessed, blessed by hardship and blessed by good fortune. And most importantly, someone believed in me.

Hanah Renstrom is in her last year at Metropolitan State University finishing the RN to BSN program. Writing has always been a passion of Hanah's. A few other interests include fitness, theology, beauty, fashion, cooking, and travel.

Rickle Dickle Sour Pickle Waldo

Samantha Bright

Rickle Dickle Sour Pickle Waldo sleeps on the floor. We bought him a bed, but he refuses it. He keeps the lights on. He never turns the TV off.

You must never wake him. When you do, he sits straight up and lets loose a terrible, howling roar at the past, eyes piercing through time itself, body and mind raging against the injustice and horrors of war. When left to awaken on his own, he will claw to consciousness ready to fight, growling if he catches himself in time, thrashing wildly if he doesn't. I think he sleeps on the floor because it's the only place he cannot fall from, no matter how he flails and shouts.

Rick will not vote. If pressed on this matter, which is not advisable, he will eventually, in a thunderous boom, declare that voting doesn't matter because, "Politicians do whatever the fuck they want anyway!" Rickle Dickle will not get on a plane. If pressed on this matter, which is not advisable, he will eventually erupt with a primal snarl: "I'm not getting on any goddamn plane! The last time I got on a plane they sent me to fuckin' Vietnam!"

"Fuckin' Vietnam!" He bellows this phrase, an accusation, a curse, an epithet, laced with a depth of venom and hatred deeper than any other I have ever witnessed.

His job in the war was to retrieve the bodies—or the largest pieces—so mothers and fathers could have a piece of their own soul presented to them cold and dead, a fait accompli.

One of those bodies was his high school best friend. No one comes back from that whole.

I speak about him in the present tense, because even in memory, he feels so vibrant and alive to me. But it is a lie.

The truth is harsher: he is gone. He lived, he endured, he raged … but all of that belongs to the past. Rick very nearly broke completely. But he didn't.

He bent, twisted, went feral at the edges. But he didn't break.

He spent the years after Vietnam hitchhiking across America, collecting his treasures: old newspapers, twisted hangers, deflated basketballs, shoes with no mate. He would go to yard sales, auctions, or simply pull over on the side of the road to go through the abandoned heaps of miscellany. He would, suddenly and swiftly, pluck something from the middle of the pile and present it to the gleaming sun, victoriously declaring, "One man's trash is another man's treasure!"

When you got close enough to see what he was holding, invariably it was a broken bike chain or a stained coat missing three buttons.

When my father found himself single, alone, trying to raise four small children, he called Rick, an old college roommate, and asked for help. Rick showed up that same week. He knocked on the door, and I, two or three years old, answered.

"Is your father home?" he asked.

He became part of our family that day, and I was never alone again.

Rick was well educated and spoke in something resembling poetry or aphasia, depending on how deeply you listened. He'd say things that sounded absurd until second or third consideration, when they suddenly began to a crooked kind of sense.

"I went to Santa Monica to hobo with the hobos," he once said, "and I out-hoboed them all!"

When asked his opinion on a meandering anecdote, he'd shrug and say: "That was an interesting play, but I'm not sure I'd read it again."

Rickle Dickle Sour Pickle didn't care about being understood. To adults, Rickle Dickle Sour Pickle Waldo seemed lost. They were puzzled by Rick and quickly dismissed him. They seemed to forget about him completely, like a half-remembered dream.

To a child, he seemed magic.

He believed the world was full of hypocrisy, cruelty, and noise. And yet, he always had something to give.

When we ran out of milk and I poured his coffee cream over my cereal like the little goblin I was, he never told me to stop.

When I toddled over from the bookshelf, holding my own treasure, and plopped down beside him, I would demand, "Read this!" with the confidence of a young princess. When we reached the end, I'd flip the front cover, and demand, "Again!" That's what I remember most about him: how generous he was. He always said yes.

Yes to another story. Yes to the park. Yes to the library. Yes to macaroni and cheese. He couldn't sleep in darkness, but he was a light to me.

He was an alcoholic and a chain-smoker, but I never begrudged him that. He was a kind drunk, a kind man. Once, when I was eight, the night before Easter, he passed out on the kitchen floor. The next morning, when I asked why he slept on the kitchen floor, he leaned in conspiratorially, eyes glittering, and whispered, "I was trying to catch the Easter Bunny." He placed tiny bets on horse races—"feeding the horsies"—and when he won, he treated us to pastries or fast-food feasts.

You never knew what Rick was going to say. I'm not sure he did either. Once, out of nowhere during a mundane conversation, he suddenly, energetically, interjected to accuse my sister's boyfriend of being "a milk breeder!" We all stared, stunned, then burst out laughing. Rick, eyes shining, laughed hardest of all.

I wish I had written down more of what he said. His ideas were so original, so unlike anyone else's, that unless you pinned them to the page, they floated away.

He never found peace. But he gave it to a child who needed it. He could not fit into the world, so he made his own, and somehow in it, I grew up safe.

I'm sad that Rick had to float away. I miss him desperately.

I would give almost anything to hear one more effervescent, carbonated idea bubble into the air and leave the world stunned. But Rick has comforted me enough.

I like to think Rick has finally found the peace and safety he gave me.

He always said one man's trash is another man's treasure.

The world may not have known what to do with him, but I did.

Rickle Dickle Sour Pickle Waldo was my treasure.

Samantha Bright, 37, is a nontraditional student who is working toward a degree in Biochemistry after a previous Bachelor's in Psychology. She is likely to be found at local art fairs, book or craft stores, or coffee shops, or in public asking strangers if she may pet their dog.

PART III: FICTION

I Stop at the Roses

Kit Renard

One after the other my feet connect with the pavement for the umpteenth time. This last stretch takes me up a hill that runs along a stretch of busy street. I am so close to home I can taste it. I stop to brush my hands through some lush coral and canary roses. The bright colors and heavy perfume enchant me. My watch starts to buzz and ask if I have finished my workout. Begrudgingly, I return to putting one foot in front of the other and carry on.

Climbing up the hill, I can just make out an orange cat that is cowering in the middle of the busy street. Quivering and howling, the cat darts in one direction before dodging back the other way to avoid being hit. I dig deep into reserves I wasn't even aware of. No matter what, I must reach this cat—I cannot let them die. As I get closer, I can see a lifted fire-engine-red truck that would be more at home in a monster truck show than on the road. As I sprint toward the cat, I can hear my track coach in my head.

*****

"Whenever you run, you are running toward something or away from something. It is up to you to decide which." My track coach continued his speech, but those words took up all the bandwidth that I had. Tumbling around in my mind all I could think was that I would never stop running. I joined track on a whim to get away from my tormentors both at home and in school. Flying across the track field I was free. No one could touch me. No one could hurt me. I was invincible.

*****

A deafening cry comes from the truck as it charges toward its prey. The cat starts to tremble in place as the truck gets ever closer. I push, oblivious to the five and a half miles I have just run. My mind may be unaware, but my muscles beg to differ. I bolt into the traffic, flailing my arms and screaming for the truck to stop. All this seems to do is encourage the truck to accelerate, focusing solely on its quarry.

I am finding it harder and harder to breathe. I put my head down and push myself to continue; there is only about half a block between me and the cat. I look up and see that I am going to be too late. One final yowl escapes the cat as it attempts to flee; the truck swerves to match the direction; moments later the truck is driving past me. The horn blares, two flags blowing in the wind, celebrating the victory—Trump 2020 on the left and the Confederate flag on the right. I cannot help but think about the last time I felt this way.

*****

Sixteen, homeless, and running. I am all the way in Portland, Oregon. I never thought I would be able to do anything but live in North Dakota. I did everything I could to put the people who hurt me as far away as possible. I needed to find somewhere I could be me and not be afraid. My coach in my head again: Did I run away from North Dakota, or did I run toward something new?

*****

I don't even recognize the sound that comes from me as I reach what is left of the cat. I continue to keen as I see that the truck didn't have the mercy to end the animal's life. The cat attempts to breath, and all that happens is wet coughs. The sight before me more fitting of a crime scene. I bend down, and a small hiss escapes the ravaged animal. I scoop them up in my arms and carry them to the grass and set the cat down as gently as I can.

I curl up next to the cat and lie there as their pants become fewer and more stretched out. I know that ending the cat's life would be a kindness, but I cannot bring myself to do it. Instead, I cry and surround them using my body to shield the cat from the world while I let them die. A few people walk past and ask if I am okay; I ignore them and continue to keen.

*****

My coach is still in my ear, "Why do you run, Steven?" I'm thirty years old, and I'm in a new city every couple of years. I am in San Antonio this time. I run six miles every morning and every evening. It's the first place that I can run every day of the year outside. Maybe this is what I have been running toward.

*****

The cat crosses over the rainbow bridge and is at peace. I have no idea how long I have been here, though. The sun starts to set, painting the sky in shades of pink and yellow, almost the same colors as the roses this morning. I do not have any tears left; I walk the rest of the way oblivious to everything.

As I walk into the front door, Derek, my husband, screams and asks me, "What the hell happened? Are you okay?" He runs his hands up and down my sides and presses my chest where I held the cat. I look down and see what all the fuss is about. A Jackson Pollock of blood, fur, and innards covers my once-white tank top.

"I am fine. I tried to save a cat on the road, but I was too late, and the cat was run over. The guy actually swerved so that he could hit the cat. He went out of his way to kill a defenseless

animal. WHAT THE FUCK IS WRONG WITH PEOPLE!"
He hugs me and pushes my head into his shoulder.

*****

I am coming up to the final hill on my run. I stop at the roses to
clip a few, the owners of the house have set up a spot for me with
a bucket, gloves, and a pair of shears. With my roses in hand, I
run to the spot where I laid the cat to rest just a couple of weeks
prior. I lay the fresh roses down with those from the day before
and rest. The sun starts to set, and the sky is alight with hues of
pink and yellow. A bittersweet smile graces my face. A single tear
drops to the ground. I turn and get back to one foot after the
other hitting the pavement.

*Kit Renard is a junior in their first year at Metro State studying
Creative Writing. Kit can usually be found in a Minneapolis or
St. Paul library writing fiction or poetry but also reading; always
reading.*

The Weight of an Empty Chair

Jewels Leepalao

The house had grown too quiet, though quiet was never meant to be unnatural. Silence was supposed to soothe, to cradle the weary heart. But this silence was sharp and brittle—a kind of absence that pressed against the ribs like a hidden shard of glass.

He moved through the rooms with care, as though each object might splinter if disturbed. The table was still set for two—though it had been days, weeks, since anyone sat across from him. Dust had begun to gather on the untouched plate, thin as a veil of frost. He told himself he would clear it away tomorrow, and tomorrow never came.

The chair remained where she had last pulled it out, angled just slightly toward him, as if in mid-conversation. Sometimes, when he passed by too quickly, he imagined she might still be there, her presence soft as candlelight. He never looked too long. Staring only revealed the wooden frame, the vacant cushion, the truth.

In his most tortuous nights, he dreamt of her voice. It arrived not in words but in cadence—the gentle rise and fall of her velvety speech, the small pause she took before answering a question, as if she handled each question with care. He woke in the dark, heart hammering, chasing that half-remembered melody, only to find the ceiling staring blankly back. The neighbors had stopped knocking. Their casseroles congealed in his freezer, stacked like monuments to their pity. He could not bear their eyes, which spoke without speaking: How long will you carry this? How long before you let her go? He wondered if love could ever be let go of, if grief had a finish line, and if he would even want to cross it.

One quiet evening, as twilight poured violet through the window, he lit a single candle on the table. Its flame swayed with the rhythm of his breath, and he sat, hands folded, and waited. Not for her return—he had surrendered that hope long ago—but for something smaller, something quieter: The feeling that she was not entirely gone.

The candle burned lower, and wax bled in rivulets, pooling at the base. He closed his eyes. Memory unfurled—her laugh, the way it began timidly and then spilled out, startling even herself. He let it echo in the hollow of his chest, and for the first time in weeks, his mouth curved upward, barely, trembling.

When the flame finally guttered, the room surrendered again to darkness. Yet it was not the same kind of silence that followed. It was gentler now, less jagged. A silence that did not cut but held.

The chair across from him was still empty. It would always be empty. But he realized, with a slow ache, that emptiness could be inhabited—not by her body, but by the immensity of what they had shared. And in that revelation, the silence softened into something almost holy. He rose, carefully pushed the chair back in, and for the first time, he cleared the plate.

Jewels Leepalao is a fourth-year Psychology major and Creative Writing minor at Metro State. She loves writing pieces that make others feel, whether that is pain or love, and often dreams of a day where she can walk into a bookstore and see her books on the shelves.

Coming Up Roses

Tara Flaherty Guy

Charlie was pouring sweat in the hot sun. Heat shimmered up off the asphalt, and shards of sunlight sparked off the chrome of his wheelchair, nearly blinding him, even with his shades on. Despite the heat, he felt chilled—way deep down inside. Always. The constantly cold thing, the doc said, was the otherwise symptomless kidney failure at work.

Consequently, in mid-August, smoking in the nursing home parking lot offered the worst of both goddamned worlds, he thought—shivering until his teeth clacked and sweating buckets. He took the last drag off his Seneca Red 100 and flicked it to the pavement. A fat drop of sweat rolled down his face and dripped off his shaggy Fu Manchu mustache onto his grubby sweatpants. His scarred bald head with its fringe of bottle-blond hair gleamed in the merciless sun.

"Got one for me?" Jimmy was wheeling up, pointing at the smoldering cigarette butt.

"Thought you said they were cheap shit," Charlie replied.

Jimmy shrugged with a sheepish grin. "You know what they say about beggars," he said.

"Don't I, though," said Charlie, tossing him the pack.

"Light me up too, Hulk," said Jimmy, wheeling closer and gesturing for the cheap Bic lighter. Charlie had picked up the Hulk nickname not long after being dumped here, thanks to his striking resemblance to the old WWE wrestler. Both he and the Hulk sported long fringes of white-blond hair, luxuriant mustaches, muscle shirts and faded do-rags; both had also been rode hard and put away wet, Charlie figured. He didn't mind the nickname.

"Gimme that lighter back when you're done. You got my last three, ya fuckin' klepto," Charlie growled at Jimmy.

He was surrounded by beggars in this place, and moochers, everybody lifting or grifting something off you. In here, pretty much everybody's money—if they had any—went to the state; Medicaid was paying for most of their ride, leaving them with a pittance of an allowance. Even the few with money had nowhere to spend it. There was nothing to buy. They needed a goddamned commissary in this joint, Charlie thought suddenly.

Meantime he'd have to talk Fern into buying him another carton of the cheap-ass shitty Seneca Reds, the way everybody freeloaded off him. Then he'd listen to her bitch about how he shouldn't be smoking with COPD. *No-duh, genius,* he thought.

It wasn't that his sister wasn't generous, he'd allow that much. Christ, if he wanted for anything, she went out of her way to provide it, from socks and underwear up to and including the big-screen TV she'd just had delivered for him. No, it was that he was sick and tired of having to ask her for money for *everything.* Why should he need to ask for money to buy a pack of Skittles, like a little kid waiting for allowance day? What a comedown. He used to *be* somebody.

A decorated homicide detective in his day, he had made damn good money, with the promise of a more-than-comfortable pension to live off in his old age. But after Wife Number Three decamped following his drunken motorcycle accident, his sister stuck him into this goddamned concentration camp for feeble old fucks, and he had lost any semblance of autonomy. This included not only his ability to wipe his own ass, or take a bath solo, or make a dirty martini or shrimp scampi at midnight if he felt like it, but also the complete and utter lack of access to his own money. It was spoken for, elsewhere. All of it.

After the bike crash that left him wheelchair bound with a traumatic brain injury, Fern—and the world at large—had agreed that Charlie needed "assistance" in daily life. Before he could say, "Well fuck me to hell," he was installed in this assisted living facility, with what was left of his pension (after dividing it between himself and two of his three ex-wives) being confiscated by the State of Minnesota for his keep. Nice payback after working his ass off for 30 years, putting his life on the line, and locking up some seriously bad actors, including at least a half dozen stone-cold killers. Not to mention getting permanent, excruciating sciatica from wearing the damn gun belt while sitting staked out for hours—or even days.

It wasn't even that he wanted the money to buy contraband or illicit items that management prohibited on premise (though he frequently wondered if they'd draw the line at a call girl ringing the front doorbell after visiting hours). It was more the principle of the thing. He wanted his own damn money, to spend how he saw fit, up to and including—yeah, let's just say it—cheap, perfumed feminine companionship for an hour if he wanted, free of judgement or second-guessing from his sister or the Gestapo that ran this place. What passed for feminine pulchritude on the premises were slim pickings, he thought glumly.

"Hey. Let's go," Jimmy said, interrupting Charlie's irritable ruminations. "Lunch is served, mon sewer," he said, tapping his watch to indicate noon. Charlie rolled his eyes at Jimmy's bungled try at *monsieur*.

"Who are you, the fuckin' maître d'?" he snapped, but began to wheel himself behind Jimmy toward the building, wondering what gastronomic horror the dining room would produce for lunch. A baloney sandwich if it was his lucky day. He paused with Jimmy at the big double doors of the dining room, but the aroma of today's salmon croquettes and tater tots made him want to retch. "Gonna take a rain check," he told Jimmy, who shrugged and rolled away toward their table.

Wheeling himself to his apartment, Charlie began to ponder ways in which he might profit by his situation, which he coldly calculated included the fact that he was younger, smarter, and more physically able than the other residents—not a high bar. He used to be a resourceful guy, able to spot opportunity, a think-outside-the-box man. He suddenly remembered a mantra from one of his early-day entrepreneurship training conferences, way back when he still had Wife Number Two and the kiddies and was trying to augment his city cop salary. The little faux marble plaque used to hang on his wall at the PD: "Be observant, see a need, fill it!"

That. Yeah, *that*! Among the wheelchair-bound oldsters he sat smoking with every day in the parking lot, he was beginning to see there was an ocean of unmet needs he could tap into. He would become a procurer and provider to the others trapped in this not-so-funny farm. The guy who could get you anything—like Radar O'Reilly on M*A*S*H, but with considerably more profit margin built into his operation.

Cigarettes … booze … weed … dirty magazines … endless possibilities began dawning on him as he considered the litany of things from the outside that his melancholy companions claimed to miss the most. He considered his potential customer base. His clientele would necessarily be a slim segment of the mostly doddering residents, he reflected—a tiny hunk at the center of the oldster Venn diagram.

His customers would have to retain some semblance of a life-spark, maybe some umbrage at their imprisonment, a desire for self-direction. They'd have to be culled from the largely obedient geriatric herd, and be willing rule-breakers, able to keep their big bazoos shut. Most of all, they'd need plenty of spending money. He wasn't gonna get sucked into some bleeding heart charity operation.

Yeah, baby. Oh *yeah*, he thought. This could get lucrative. All he needed was a reliable contact on the outside—he still knew people on the street—and a group of regular customers to fleece on the inside. Sheeple to be sheared, he thought with an inward grin.

He let himself into his apartment, rolling over the threshold with a bump. For the first time in months, a faint gleam of hope shimmered on the periphery of his grim outlook. Easing himself from his wheelchair into his recliner, he leaned back and closed his eyes, an uncharacteristic faint smile on his face. His breathing slowed, then grew regular. As he slipped toward sleep, the strains of an old show tune began echoing through his mind. "Everything's coming up roses ..."

Yeah baby. Roses for Charlie—finally. Money of his own, maybe even somebody to spend it on. As sleep came stealing, he drifted off, dreaming of the gleam of high heels and the faint scent of Tigress cologne stirring the stale air of his room.

Tara Flaherty Guy obtained her BA in Creative Writing in 2018 from Metro State University in St. Paul, where she was born and raised, and still lives and writes. Since then her work has been published in St. Paul Almanac, Remington Review, Emerge Literary Journal, and Longridge Review, among many others.

Morning Cigarette

Eponine Diatta

The mattress shifted as Stan crawled out of bed that morning. I'd been up for hours, watching the sun creep up over the neighbor's roof with my back turned to my husband.

Most nights had been like this since we moved in. I'd squeeze my eyes shut trying to fall asleep before the deep, heavy sinking in my stomach forced them open again. Stan would roll over in the night and reach out, trying to pull me closer. Each time my body crept to the edge of the bed away from his arms, as if we were two magnets of the same pole. It was an energetic repulsion that I couldn't push through. I heard a pan on the stove, then keys, then the front door opening and closing. He'd gone for cigarettes. I'd told him the night before that he'd run out, but surely, the wine washed his mind clean of any memory of it, like it always does. Maybe I should've mentioned it earlier, before he opened the bottle.

I looked around our bedroom, now fully illuminated. The bare walls and sharp-edged Ikea furniture made it feel as cold and artificial as a showroom. Besides one photo—a framed moment from our wedding night, our cheeks pressed together, smiling into the camera—there was no evidence anyone lived here, much less two people in love.

It hadn't always been that way. Our old apartment had been brimming with signs of life. Shelves full of knickknacks and worn hardcover books and photos of our friends and family. The coffee table was often covered in loose screws and Allen wrenches and half-done sketches. Stan liked to start things he couldn't finish, a trait that would've been aggravating in anyone but him. He was a dreamer; I was a doer. That was us.

Back then I'd put on records for us to sing along to as we cooked one of his improvised dinner recipes, giving each other tastes from the hot wooden spoon. The apartment was so small we'd trip over the other's feet when we danced between the stove and the fridge. At night we'd climb into bed and hold each other close, fingers and arms and legs linked so tightly it felt like we'd been fused together. Our chests rose and fell in sync, breathing as one big fleshy being.

I can't remember when it started to change, exactly. Maybe it was when Stan got promoted and started coming home later and later. Maybe it was when I started putting my phone on Do Not Disturb during the day and missed his calls. Maybe it was months later, when I would start finding empty liquor bottles at the bottom of the trash can, covered in ripped-up paper towels. Maybe it was when I started hiding bottles of my own. All I knew is when Stan told me he had put a down payment on a fixer-upper in North Minneapolis, I felt like I'd had shackles slapped onto my wrists.

He showed me a picture of this old, dilapidated, blue nightmare of a house that sank into the dead, overgrown yard. "It'll be work, but it's an investment, right? In our future," he said.

I saw what was ahead. Both of our names on a mortgage. Nights spent retiling a bathroom or washing baseboards or bouncing a fussy, snotty baby on my hip while Stan drank and rambled on about his next project. Another one he'd never finish, one I'd end up finishing for him. What I couldn't see was myself, happy in that ugly house with him. I wanted to say it, but my mouth couldn't form the words. They were trapped in my throat, sticky and suffocating.

And then I was there. He would drone on about what kind of life we'd have in the house, and it sounded so flat and so false.

A house, a baby, such bland nonspecifics I could place on two abstract stick figures in my mind but never on him and me.

"Vera, you can leave, you know," my mom told me, her hand holding mine tracing circles on my palm with her thumb. Suddenly her fingertips were hot as cinders, singeing my skin. I pulled away.

I had had breakfast with my mom days before. Over eggs and toast all the words came up and fell out of my mouth. All of my dissatisfactions spilled onto the table.

"We're married."

"But do you still love him?"

I opened my mouth to answer, but then the server came to fill our mugs and the words had left me.

I was thinking about my mom's hands when I noticed the air in the bedroom had started to look gray and hazy. It was only when the shriek of the fire alarm pierced my ears that I realized it was smoke, crawling under the door and into the room. Coughing, I pressed my hand to the door and my palms were hot again. I turned back to the window, opened it and slipped out. I stepped back, letting my feet take me all the way to the fence.

From where I stood I saw no flames. Just big solid clouds of black smoke spilling out and up and into the air. Sirens wailed somewhere as I watched the edges of the windows become charred. Barefoot in the mud, I was finally cooling down and the pit in my stomach was gone. Maybe I'd left it in bed. Maybe I needed to leave Stan.

Eponine (Nina) Diatta is in her first year at Metro State as a Professional Communications major. She is a multidisciplinary writer and performer who, in her free time, can be found hogging the TouchTunes at dive bars across the Twin Cities.

A Mother Against the Dead World

Ximena Castillo Perez

The subtle discomfort had evolved by the time the sun began setting. She now knew that her labor had started. Lizzy leaned against the rusted frame of an abandoned truck. The pain came in waves, hot and deep, curling through her spine, sweat dripping from her hair despite the cold.

"Not yet," she whispered, pressing her hand to her swollen belly. "Please, not yet." The highway stretched before her, broken and silent. Cars had long ago been stripped for parts or left to rot, their windows clouded with dirt and old blood, some even broken by those who had looked for supplies. She'd been walking for two days, surviving on a single can of peaches and the hope that the old hospital marked on her map hadn't been burned to the ground or ransacked of all equipment.

The last time she had been near people was weeks ago. Back then, there had been eight of them, survivors who clung together more out of fear than trust. Among them had been Mary, another pregnant woman, further along than Lizzy. Mary had believed they could rebuild something, the baby inside her filling her with hope. She'd smiled at every sunrise, no matter how gray.

But when her time came, no one knew what to do. No doctors, no clean water, no antiseptic. Lizzy had held her hand as she bled out on the dirty mattress that others had scavenged months ago, her cries muffled by a dirty rag in her mouth. By the time Mary's son had arrived to what was left of the world, she was gone. Her body lay lifeless on the mattress. A river of blood began between her legs. The baby was quick to follow his mother. Almost as if he could feel Mary's absence, he began crying, bringing panic to all in the group. In the end, it was a man named Alex who had the courage to do what was "needed." He smothered the infant when his crying drew the infected to their hiding place. Lizzy could still hear the small, strangled sound, and Alex's broken whisper: "I'm sorry." She'd left the group the next morning. Better to die alone than live among people who had learned to kill hope.

Now, another contraction gripped her, harder than before. She dropped to her knees, panting through closed teeth. The baby was coming soon. She scanned the horizon, long rows of trees at each side of the road. Then she saw it: a farmhouse half-collapsed, its roof sagging, but the barn beside had no signs of the dead being near. Lizzy forced herself to her feet and stumbled forward. Every step sent knives of pain through her back. Her breath came in gasps.

She reached the barn and slipped inside, latching the door behind her. Dust filled her lungs, and the smell of rot clung to everything. She found a corner with old hay and tattered blankets and sank down, shaking. Her fingers trembled as she pulled a small knife from her bag. The same knife she'd used to cut food, to fend off the desperate, to survive.

When the next contraction came, she screamed into her sleeve. No one would hear, she told herself. No one human, at least. Hours passed, minutes maybe, time no longer made sense. The pain grew worse, the fear sharper. She thought of Mary and what Alex had done. She thought of the world that used to be, where women didn't have to give birth in barns haunted by the dead. The sound of her breath echoed off the wooden walls. Her body fought, trembled, gave way. She thought she might die there, nameless and forgotten.

And then—silence. She blinked through the sweat, the blur of tears, the haze of exhaustion. In her arms lay the child—small, still, covered in the mess of birth and blood. For one terrible moment, she thought it hadn't survived. Then its chest rose. A breath. No cry.

The baby only stared—eyes half-open, dark and unblinking, its tiny mouth closed as if it somehow understood.

The silence wrapped around them both. Outside, nothing stirred. Lizzy let out a shuddering breath.

"You know," she whispered, brushing a trembling finger along its cheek. "You know not to make a sound."

She cleaned the baby as best she could, wrapped it tight, and held it against her chest. The quiet pressed in, almost sacred. But as the night wore on, she began to wonder if the silence was a mercy or an omen.

In the dark, she thought she heard movement beyond the barn walls—slow, dragging steps. But still, the baby did not cry, not once. Not when the door creaked, not when she held her breath, knife in hand. The child only stared, calm and knowing, its heartbeat soft against hers.

When the noise outside faded, Lizzy dared to look down. The baby's eyes were still open. Watching her. And in their depths, she saw something she couldn't name—something far too old, too aware for a newborn.

Lizzy held the child closer, her whisper trembling: "You're not supposed to understand, little one." But the baby did not blink, and it did not cry. Lizzy smiled down at the baby, with new hope igniting in her chest.

Ximena Castillo Perez is set to graduate from Metro State in 2026 with a BA in Studio Arts and a minor in Creative Writing. They currently spend most of their time writing, painting, playing video games, and helping to manage their father's company in Minneapolis.

Heart-Shaped Box

Jackson Michael

He wrapped his fingers around the lid and gently opened the top of his little box. Out floated a glowing red heart that glittered in the morning sunlight like a ruby. It wasn't like a heart you might find in one of us, a muscled mass of arteries and chambers. It was a perfectly shaped Valentine's card heart that a child might draw.

Rowan snapped the lid closed quickly so no more of the little gems escaped. There was no knowing how many of the magic hearts he had, so it was important not to waste them. He reached up and tried to catch the heart as it floated away, but as his hand got close, it popped like a bubble and was gone.

Rowan was left in the meadow alone with the grass and flowers of orange and yellow and red, swaying gently in the early dew-covered breeze. A little caterpillar crawled, meandering, up the side of a tree, and a bird's song rose with the sun's rays, welcoming the new day.

As he cradled the box in his hands, he pondered what it all could mean. He had no idea where it had come from. When he'd woken up that morning, it had been there on the night-stand next to his bedside. A little brown wooden chest with no lock or latch or key, as if its contents were not meant to be kept hidden away.

Thankful for the supposed gift, Rowan had grabbed the box and carefully padded through the hall and out the front door barefoot so he'd not wake anyone up. Though that was only half the truth, since he'd also been so excited that he'd forgotten his shoes in the first place. A happy accident.

He loved running through the clover-dusted meadow without his shoes on, though Mother certainly gave him an earful every time she caught him doing it. Maybe he could give her a heart so she wouldn't be mad.

"Rowan, breakfast!" He heard from back at his house up on the hill.

He'd have to figure out how many hearts he had later. He shoved the box into the large pocket on the front of his overalls and scampered through the field and up the hill back home, trying to knock off as much mud as he could along the way. He came in through the back door and immediately noticed the pancakes on the kitchen table, steaming and fluffy, with butter melting down the sides.

"Ah, ah, ah," he heard his mother say from somewhere near, most likely some hidden perch. "Where are your shoes, mister? Wipe those grubby feet on the mat."

Such sharp eyes! Rowan thought.

She was standing in her nice blue dress with a dark blue apron that she was drying her hands with. It looked like she was just finishing washing some dishes. Rowan hoped he never had to wash any dishes; it didn't seem like much fun. Though the bubbles, on the other hand, looked like a lot of fun.

"Mother, I have something for you." He tried to deflect as he pulled out the box. His tentative fingers opened the lid, and a sparkling heart floated up and out. He snapped the lid closed again quickly so no more would escape.

The little heart drifted toward his mother, who bent down and cupped her hands around it. Rowan tried to warn her about it popping if you got too close to it but was too slow. And to his astonishment it didn't pop but radiated in her hands, growing in strength until it bathed her whole face in a soft red glow.

"Oh, it's beautiful my dear—thank you. I love you," she said.

Rowan felt like his own heart was growing or glowing or at least full of warmth too. He couldn't help but smile from ear to ear. His mother held the heart close to her chest, and it seemed to dissolve into her.

"Now go wipe the mud off and come back in and eat." *She remembered!* Rowan thought, mouth falling open in silent protest, though there was nothing to do but comply.

So, they didn't get you out of trouble, good to know. But the feeling that they did give, after giving a heart away and seeing the joy on his mother's face, that was a gift in and of itself. How many of these did he have? Could he make his whole family happy?

"Big questions can't be answered on an empty stomach," he recited, remembering what his grandfather had told him. Guess they'd have to wait.

He devoured the pancakes as if it was his last meal, or first meal, whichever you prefer, and made a list of all the people he could share his hearts with. Hopefully he'd have enough for them all. The box wasn't all that big, so based on the size of the hearts, he estimated he had about four left.

He could give one each to Grandma and Grandpa, then one to Dad, and there would still be one for Fred the dog. His sister would have to go without one. Those are the sacrifices we make though; it couldn't be helped.

After syrup coated every available surface of the dishware and Rowan's fork was able to stick to his hand even when it was turned upside down, a remarkable feat of magic indeed, he hopped down, thanked his mom with a sticky sweet hug, and ran out the door.

Back in the safety of the glade, he cracked open the little wooden box ever so slightly, trying to peek in. A heart popped out and floated up before he could close the lid again, stopping the flow. Boy, they were quick little buggers. It had almost looked like the box was still full though. It had to be a trick of the eye. Now that another one had escaped, he would have to cut someone else out. Maybe his grandparents could share one.

Rowan clutched the box tightly and ran back up to the house to find his father. He heard a noise in the garage as he got closer and decided to check there. As he rounded the old rusted car that had been overgrown with grass and flowers, he could see that the door was open and his father was inside working on an old radio.

"Is it broken?" Rowan asked, walking in.

"It was, but this should just about do it." His father sat hunched over a small workbench with a single-bulbed light hanging above him that reflected off the different tools hanging on the wall. As he connected a loose wire and turned a knob, the radio sprang to life and spouted an old classical tune.

"Ah-ha!" His father exclaimed.

Rowan smiled, catching his father's infectious joy that had spilled over and splashed about the tiny workbench. In the moment, he forgot about trying to be stingy and lifted the lid to his box. One, two, three hearts popped out and Rowan felt startled by how many and how quickly they had escaped. But as he glanced in he could see that, sure enough, the box had refilled itself.

He closed the lid so they didn't all get away as the three he'd let out floated toward his father.

"For me?" His father said, holding out his hands and cradling the tiny hearts.

"Yes," Rowan stated proudly.

"Oh, they are wonderful, my son. Thank you."

And just like before, the glow brightened, filling the garage and melding into his father. Rowan was suddenly wrapped in a giant hug and lifted into the air. And he sank into the comfort and safety of his father's strong arms as he was twirled to the music. He heard his father laugh and added his own laughter to the chorus. He felt like he was the most valuable thing in the world and there wasn't any room left in him for fears or worries.

And to top it all off, his box had been full again! Fine. His sister could have one too. In fact, he could share with the whole town. He didn't need to worry about running out at all if the box could refill itself.

"I love you, Dad," Rowan said.

"I love you too, Son!" His father replied, finally setting him back down.

"I gotta go. I have more hearts to give out," Rowan said. He felt his own heart filled to the brim, as if it were ready to overflow or burst from his own chest.

"Okay, and Rowan?" His father said, putting a big hand on his shoulder and crouching down, coming face to face with him.

"Yes?" Rowan asked.

"I'm proud of you."

Rowan saw the truth of that statement in his father's eyes and felt like he'd grown ten feet taller.

"I need to share this with everybody," Rowan said with determination.

"Well go on then," his father nodded to him.

Rowan burst from the garage, ran down the drive and continued down the street to his grandparents' house, giving hearts to each of them. He gave one to Fred the stray dog and, yes, even one to his sister.

He learned that if he was stingy or too picky, then he would run out, as if the box was refilling based on the love he had in his own heart and not on its own accord. If he didn't give them away, they'd slowly turn blue and disappear and be gone forever. Rowan was determined not to let that happen.

So, he gave some to the mailman, the grocer, and his teacher. Even the grumpy old man in the house on the corner cracked a smile when Rowan gave one to him. He gave his little hearts to anyone and everyone he met until he had shared with the whole town. The more hearts he gave away, the more he had.

And he never ran out.

Jackson Michael is currently working toward his BA through Metro's TREC program for incarcerated persons. Writing stories that remind us of our shared humanity while creating fantastic worlds to explore has given Jackson a second chance at life and a hope for the future. He believes that stories really do have the power to set each and every one of us truly free.

Waiting for the Fire

Kit Renard

Sylvie and Nina reached the clearing where the cabin stood, weatherworn but sturdy. The air hung heavy in its stillness, thick and damp. The birch trees wavered in the golden sunlight; their trunks formed an uneven fence that surrounded the clearing. With the cabin in sight, Sylvie ran toward it, arms outstretched as though the entire forest belonged to her. "It's perfect, absolutely perfect!" she yelled.

Nina took her time finishing the walk up. Their Jeep at the bottom of the hill was her only tie to civilization, so close yet so far away. "Perfect" was not the first word that came to her mind. Hell, it wasn't even the fiftieth. The ground was uneven, and her shoes sank with every step as the scent of mud competed with her lilac perfume. She loathed camping, she had since she was ten and her father took her camping to "appreciate the finer things." Twenty years later and she still hadn't forgiven him, or tents, or mosquitos for the miserable week that it was.

At least this trip would not take place in a tent. It was an inheritance—Nina's inheritance. She would not dishonor her late grandfather. She would check the place out at least once. The note said, "Two miles past the giant boulder and then up the hill you will find my cabin. Well, now your cabin." She had read it over and over and, with some convincing on the part of Sylvie, had decided that a weekend visit wouldn't be all bad. No matter what, she thought, she would get some closure. And who knows, she might even enjoy some quiet before the world got busy again.

It was their six-year anniversary. In those six years Sylvie had taken Nina skiing in Montana, surfing in Bali, and camping in

Nevada for two of the worst days of their entire relationship, but at least the views had been stunning. Sylvie loved open spaces and star-kissed skies, trying to connect to Nina the way Sylvie's father had to her before the cancer took him. Nina on the other hand preferred four walls with a roof and an internet connection. Well, that and clean sheets. Despite this, they'd still built something that felt like love. As she looked at the small, sagging roof of the cabin and the vines that strangled the porch, she wondered if opposites were built to last.

As they both stepped inside, a fog cloud of dust nearly blinded them. The air was suffused with iron and pine, two scents that don't belong together yet refused to be separated. All the furniture was covered in what was once white sheets, and the floorboards moaned with every step. In the corner, a wood stove resided next to shelves adorned with rusty tools and an oil lantern. They walked into the back room, which resembled a shed with a couple of bunk beds and windows clouded with spider silk. "It's *cute*," Sylvie squealed.

"Cute is one word for it," Nina muttered, as she brushed off the nearest countertop. "Condemned is another."

Sylvie shot her a look but didn't take the bait. Nina grabbed a broom and cleaned up enough of the area to unload their bags, and they ate rehydrated soup by gaslight. As Nina was cleaning, she spotted a leather-bound book that was untouched by the mess of the rest of the place. She reached down and picked up the small volume. It was warm to the touch, as if it had been the bed of a cat moments before.

"Sylvie," she called, sharper than she had intended.

Sylvie, who was in the other room, rushed up, rag in hand. "What?"

Nina pointed. "Someone's idea of art, I think."

Sylvie took it. "Feels real." She flipped it open. The pages were patchy, stitched together, the thread switched between red, gold, and black as she flipped through the pages. "Impressive," she said. "I wonder if your grandfather made it."

"Close it. Please." Nina all but yelled.

"Why? It's just—"

"Sylvie, p-l-e-a-s-e."

Sylvie slowly closed it and watched Nina as she waited for her to explain what had her on edge. But Nina didn't; something about it made her feel as if she were covered in bugs. Yet, it reminded her of family and the things you don't speak of, whose pressure you feel under your skin forever and always.

Later that night, rain licked at the windows, desperate for a taste of what was inside. Sylvie was bent over the stove; she insisted it would help Nina's nerves. Sylvie talked about taking longer trips up here, "now that we know how good you are at this," but Nina was too transfixed by the damn book, which seemed to exhale with each gust of wind.

Sylvie picked it up again. "You seriously don't want to know what's inside?"

"I'm good. I'd rather you threw it into that fire."

Sylvie laughed. "You are hating everything about being here, aren't you?"

"Everything out here hates me—it started it," she snapped. Silence came and consumed everything in its path, sharper than any knife or argument.

Sylvie looked down at the book. "Fine. We'll leave tomorrow."

Nina opened her mouth, but before she could apologize the lantern flickered, dimmed before it brightened up again, and then dimmed,` and so on. Each pulse matched her breath for breath. Nina noticed that the book had shifted slightly and was closer to the fire.

"Did you move it?" she asked as goosebumps raced down her arms.

"No."

The pages fluttered open of their own accord. Nina and Sylvie froze in place and stared as a face formed across the pages, like a slightly shaken Etch A Sketch, before it closed.

"What in the nine hells was that?" escaped from Sylvie's mouth as she exhaled.

"I told you," Nina whispered. "I told you I didn't want to know."

Sylvie didn't sleep. Nina half-dreamed of whispers, of her grandfather murmuring a lullaby she didn't remember learning. Each time she turned, she thought the book emanated light from its edges, like tiny veins that pumped fire.

At dawn, Sylvie sat outside on the porch as she balanced the book on her knees. Nina opened the door; the birch leaves shook as if startled.

"I saw my dad in the book," Sylvie said without meeting Nina's gaze. "You know I barely remember him. But, last night, I saw his face. He was laughing. Talking to me."

"That wasn't real," Nina said.

"I don't care if it wasn't real." The way Sylvie said it, more whole than she had ever been, yet broken, Nina realized how little she really knew the person beside her. Six years, and they'd built everything on shared space and habits, but not shared skeletons.

"Give it to me," Nina said as she reached for it. Sylvie hesitated. "Syl, please."

Nina all but wrenched the thing from Sylvie. The book was warm again; it breathed, pulsated. Nina took it inside, shoved it into the stove, and struck a match. And then another. The flames bent away from the book, refused to consume it. Nina recited the lullaby from her dream. That's when the flames gripped the book, slow but unshakeable.

Sylvie watched from the doorway. "What if it's important?"

"It is," Nina started, silent tears streamed down her cheek, "but not in the way you are thinking."

Evening came, the cabin perfumed by the fragrance of burnt honey and rain-drenched ash. Nina sat outside, wrapped in Sylvie's jacket. They didn't talk. What was there to say that wouldn't sound like smoke or a burning fire? Nina looked up at Sylvie and saw that the joy that always lit up Syl's face had dimmed. Grief or understanding took its place.

"You still hate camping?" Sylvie asked, a bit of mirth on the edges of her somber tone.

"More than ever," she giggled.

"You did agree to come."

Nina shrugged, "Yeah, because you asked me to."

Sylvie nodded. "Maybe, next time we go somewhere … less haunted."

"And that has an internet connection," Nina said, though she knew there wouldn't be a next time. Some crucial piece of them had been incinerated just as the book itself was. It left behind ash, and a strange warmth lingered.

They climbed down the hill; Nina looked back once. The cabin stood framed by the birch trees as they swayed as if in applause. At the porch railing, faint and without color, a shape leaned against the post. A man with his hands clasped together smiled as if he had always been waiting for the fire.

Kit Renard is a junior in their first year at Metro State studying Creative Writing. Kit can usually be found in a Minneapolis or St. Paul library writing fiction or poetry but also reading, always reading.

Campsite 27

Anna Stagg

The rain claps the forest foliage like rapturous applause, but each family member is tucked in and dry under a rainfly. Mom hears no sound from the tent with the rowdiest crew, ten feet away. In her tent, Little Brother is snug beside her and Little Sister beside Dad, each on their own bag and mat.

Mom flops her legs down like sandbags inside her polyester bed and sighs a smile. Her gaze rises to the nylon fabric pulled taut by crossed tent poles, sheltering them from the raindrops that slide like a thin waterfall away from their dry cocoon. Cradled by nature, covered by the maternal arms of oak and pine, no walls divide them tonight.

The rain fades into silence as if gestured by a conductor. Her whole being inhales the earthy air, and her back, hips, and shoulders release into the mat as she breathes out a rugged day's work. From the deep waters the silence breaks with a haunting song—the mating wail of the loon. The low and steady call rises on the night air, a song of longing and hope and beauty.

Her mind melts into the melody and the percussive croaks of toads. Surely these were the same specimens pursued by a two-year-old boy earlier today. Their captor held his beady-eyed treasures until those pudgy hands were needed to hunt for the perfect marshmallow skewer. Gingerly releasing them, Little Brother watched his wild friends hop safely back to their haven of marshland grass—all the while oblivious to the feasting mosquitos. But even tiny, itchy, swollen mounds of poison dotting his tender body couldn't fetter devotion to his new habitat. Her awareness returns to the soft breathing of peaceful sleepers as the loon wails again.

In the stillness she thinks of the woman they left behind just three days before. As if peering through a camera, she sees them on the porch rocker, hears the creak and whispering breeze as they glide forward and back, forward and back. Little legs dangle; a ninety-year-old throaty giggle mingles with a squeaky two-year-old one. She sees them picking daisies, filling the bird bath, checking the rain gauge. She knows he won't remember.

A few tears run down her cheek and into her ear. She turns toward her son, fine blond hair framing his plump sun-kissed cheeks and round bump of a nose, his breath steady with content. She tastes the salty droplets that are the flavor of change.

And the loon wails, beckoning with its melodious plea to rest her soul under the moon. Tonight, the black bear, the tadpole, the baby loon, the baby, the child, the mother, the father, the toad and mosquito are lulled by the comfort of one song. Tonight, the whole world is sleeping.

Anna Stagg will graduate from Metro State this spring with a BA in Individualized Studies and a minor in Creative Writing. She lives in Minneapolis with her husband and two of her four adult children.

ACKNOWLEDGMENTS

As editor, I would like to extend my sincerest gratitude to you, the reader, first and foremost. A reader who takes the time to read the acknowledgements is a truly dedicated reader, indeed. It is one thing to read a book; it is another thing to digest a book in its entirety.

For it is not just the editors or the contributors who make this dream possible, but the invisible web of united minds and hands blanketing us against the backdrop, providing the support to lean against.

That invisible web must be acknowledged, both in this anthology and in our personal lives. When thinking about resiliency, noticing one's own efforts is the starting point: We are at the forefront of our own destinies. But it is imperative that we go beyond ourselves and notice our own invisible webs in our lives. None of us got here alone. None of us will get where we are going alone.

Thank you to Metro State University for allowing *Haute Dish* to take root and grow. Thank you to Suzanne Nielsen, who, for over twenty years, fertilized and watered *Haute Dish*, allowing its vines to thicken and lengthen, expanding the publication until it reached its next stage: this anthology. Thank you to Belo Cipriani for guiding us to publication and providing us with the tools and knowledge to get the job done. Thank you to every professor and faculty member at Metro State who shared *Haute*

Dish with their students. Thank you to each editor and contributor, past and present, for your countless hours of support and dedication, passing the torch year after year to the next group of students.

Thank you to the copyeditors, James Estwick, Kit Renard, Anna Stagg and whose detailed eyes made sure each punctuation was in its appropriate place.

Thank you to my wonderful group of editors. Without your grit and heart, this anthology wouldn't exist. Thank you to Lisa Castillo, Deepa Ghalley, Meg Kosowski, Hailley Lower, Kisha Neely, Éowyn Prusak, Kit Renard, and Dodi Vessels for their work on this issue. Thank you to those editors who consistently returned to the work and helped shape it into its final form. Your ongoing presence and attention sustained this project from beginning to end.

Thank you to the library staff at Metro State for your time and support. Thank you to the Ramsey County Libraries, which housed me for countless hours as I pored over this manuscript. Thank you to my partner and children, for your endless encouragement, belief in me, tolerance and understanding of the late nights, and for bringing me copious amounts of coffee, without which none of this would have found its form.

And, finally, thank you to the contributors. Your courage and vulnerability are breathtaking. I am endlessly grateful for the hard work you poured into your pieces, and for that moment of bravery when you clicked submit. Your stories have inspired and encouraged me and will do the same for each and every reader.

–Stephanie Major, Managing Editor